THE
REFERRAL
MINDSET

Also by Kerry Johnson

New Mindset, New Results

*Why Smart People Make Dumb Mistakes
With Their Money*

Willpower

Mastering Self-Confidence with NLP

Phone Sales

Sales Magic

How to Read Your Client's Mind

Peak Performance

Trust-Based Selling

THE
REFERRAL
MINDSET

7
EASY STEPS TO
EXPLOSIVE
GROWTH FROM YOUR
OWN CUSTOMERS

KERRY JOHNSON,
MBA, PH.D.

MEDIA

Published 2021 by Gildan Media LLC
aka G&D Media
www.GandDmedia.com

FIRST EDITION 2021

Front Cover design by David Rheinhardt of Pyrographx

Interior design by Meghan Day Healey of Story Horse, LLC

Library of Congress Cataloging-in-Publication Data is available upon request

ISBN: 978-1-7225-0181-5

10   9   8   7   6   5   4   3   2   1

Contents

Introduction

What You Will Get from This Book

Have you ever had trouble getting referrals? Have you ever felt that if you were doing a great job for a client or customer, they would just volunteer business, or at least tell all their friends about you?

Referrals are the most effective way of getting business you will ever use. Our research shows that referrals are 35 percent more likely to do business with you and will give you 25 percent more money. There is absolutely no rejection. They are also flat-out fun. But if referrals are so effective and profitable, why are they so hard to get?

The answer lies in mindset. Most of my coaching clients say they were initially excited and asked everybody for referrals. But after many years of rejection and hearing, "I don't know anybody," they just gave up. The mindset now often is, "I tried asking for referrals. It doesn't work."

Many of my coaching clients tell me in the beginning of our relationship that they wish referrals were easier to get. They realize the importance of referrals, but getting them seems elusive. They don't want to be overbearing, and they feel pushy in asking. They certainly don't want to lose a sale. They are, in the end, terrified even to bring the topic up. Their mindset about referrals is the issue.

What You Will Get from This Book

In this book you will not only learn how to develop a results-focused mindset but will also learn proven techniques for gaining five to ten referrals every week. If you study the concepts here you'll never have to look for new business ever again. You will simply attract a steady stream of referrals every week. One of my coaching clients learned only one of these techniques and now gains three referrals every day. You will too.

In chapter 1, you will learn why referrals are so critically important in building your business. Research shows that clients care more about the relationship than price or fees. We will also talk about Forrester Research studies showing that clients and customers care more about feeling understood than a discount.

We will talk extensively about how you were trained to ask for referrals and why those techniques don't work. There are many ways of asking. Most professionals simply say, "Whom can you refer me to?" When a client says they don't know anybody, they are really thinking about the last time someone asked for your services in the last seven days. It's simple to say, "I can't think of anybody right now, but I talk about you to my friends all the time." This is only a filler sentence. They rarely talk about you, but they feel put on the spot and try to be polite.

Asking for referrals is mostly about elegance. It is having a conversation with a client instead of feeling you need to pitch. It is a request for a favor of mutual benefit than a one-sided, "Do something for me."

One of my tennis buddies sent a referral request through our LinkedIn connection. A lawyer turned merger and acquisition specialist, he was looking for new business. Rick and I play tennis a lot. He is a quality guy. I gave him a reflex response: "I don't know anybody." This response is the thought that people have when they feel put on the spot. I wanted to help Rick but didn't want to think that hard. Most of us remember details in conversations only from the past few days. When you ask for a referral, your client tries to remember anybody mentioning a need in the last seventy-two hours. Since they can't remember much past that, you will hear "I don't know anybody." Your clients or customers will do the same.

Referrals are based on frequency of contact, not competence. Your clients and customers know you are competent. They often don't know the difference between good enough and great. There is a big difference between a good and great speaker. The great ones do three things:

1. They are very entertaining.
2. They convey content audiences can use immediately.
3. They utilize great participation. Audiences feel part of the program instead of just being lectured to.

Very few speakers do these things (I obviously feel I do), but audience participants know a good speaker when they hear one. They aren't bored, uninterested, or distracted. When they hear a good speaker, they are impressed. But when they hear a great speaker, do they really value the difference enough to give referrals? The answer is generally no.

Speakers who are merely good enough can get referrals if they keep up frequency of contact. They follow up with the meeting planner after the event. They call a few months later to catch up. This is how good speakers get more referrals than great speakers who don't engage after the event.

How much is a customer or client worth over the course of a lifetime relationship? Is it the price of a transaction? Is it revenue based on the years of the relationship, incorporating repeat sales? The answer is the value of that relationship and the referrals your client brings to you.

Network marketing is an amazing concept. Often marketers make a sale and ask their customer for ten names of people they know. It is a great model but is often done in a very inelegant way. Your mindset should utilize the same network marketing model, but with more elegance. You should see the value of a customer not only in the business they bring, but in the accumulation of the referrals they produce.

In chapter 2 we will talk about three kinds of mindsets in creating a constant stream of referrals. First, we will talk about the fixed-growth mindset. Fixed-mindset people believe in static intelligence and growth. They believe the abilities they currently have will never grow or improve. They argue about commissions and fight over leads. They struggle to take their slice of a limited amount instead of growing the size of the pie.

Growth-mindset people look at setbacks as new opportunities. Their attitude is one of becoming better, learning more, and a constant journey toward growth.

The second type of mindset is inward versus outward. The inward-mindset person thinks only of how their actions impact themselves. The outward-mindset person thinks about how their actions impact others; they also tend to be fairer and more generous.

The third element is called the results-focused mindset. This refers to the ability to change mindset in an attempt to reach one's goals. People of this type realize that the mindset they have now will generate the same results, but changing how they think about activities, interactions, and communication will generate more success in reaching goals and will improve results. This mindset is important, because you are perfectly set up for the success you currently have. The only way you will be able to produce better results is to change your mindset.

I once told a coaching client making $100,000 a year that he would have to double his hours to double the income to $200,000 a year. He said he was already working sixteen-hour days. There was no more time left. I asked how many hours he worked and what his income was over the last five years. He said eight to ten hours a day, and his income has been static at $100,000. That proved my point. Unless you improve your skill set, your income won't grow. The same thing is true with mindset. Unless you improve your mindset, your outcomes will stay the same.

Why Your Mindset Is Critical

I am often asked why mindset is so important. It simply boils down to how you think. It is the way you address your goals, relationships, and the future, as well as how you evaluate the past.

One of my clients, Carlos, spent time with me creating a new weekly business plan. He discovered how much activity was needed to hit weekly, monthly, and annual goals. Next, we organized how many clients and prospects he needed to talk to. The third week we focused on a tool I call the *five-step bridge*. It's a very useful method, which shows the producer how to listen to clients and customers. It boils down to "listening people into buying." Using this system correctly results in a 38 percent closing ratio. It gets clients and prospects to tell you what they want and then focuses them on committing to a solution.

The problem is getting the producer to listen. Most of my clients initially have a self-sabotaging mindset. They think sales is about persuading people to buy. But an effective sales process is really about asking questions. It's about finding goals, wants, and desires. It's about structuring the conversation to make people feel understood instead of pushing them to understand. Sales is really about "listening people" into doing things that are right for them.

It's not enough to teach sales skills. My clients first have to learn how to listen. Everyone thinks they listen well. Few do. Listening well takes a change in mindset, which is much more difficult than learning a new sales skill set.

Think in Terms of Building a Business

One aspect of mindset is to always be thinking in terms of business development. No matter what industry you're in, this process should always be at the top of your mind. That doesn't mean you need to cold-call every day, or even make social media posts three times a week (although that is a good idea). It means to consistently listen for opportunities.

Building your business is really about possessing a growth mindset. Many of my clients are tired of being told to ask for referrals. They are burned out from hearing, "I don't know anyone." But when a client mentions names of their friends, family, and colleagues, a growth-mindset person might think, "I should find out more about these people. Maybe could help them!" Learning a few phrases will not help. Having a 3 x 5 card paper-clipped to the file reminding you to ask for referrals is better than nothing. But possessing a business growth mindset will always help you attune yourself to new opportunities.

Referrals Don't Get Better with Age

Referrals are not like fine wine or aged cheese. The longer they sit, the sourer they get. Often I hear clients brag about getting a few referrals. Perhaps they reach out to book an appointment, but most of the time they just put them in a drawer. When business gets slow, they call the lead, having forgotten nearly everything about this person. This also speaks to mindset. A growth mindset values a referral opportunity and acts quickly. The source of your referral also wants to know the result of the lead they gave you. If they think you failed to follow up, your source will quickly dry up.

Asking for Referrals: A Mix of Skills, Confidence, and Mindset

It's not enough to learn how to ask for referrals. It's much more important to have a growth mindset. When you consistently think about building your business with referrals, applying the skills necessary to be successful will be much easier. I often hear that producers fail to ask because they forget, or they don't want to lose rapport by asking. There is a big difference between awkwardly asking for a name and mentioning how much you value client relationships. It's a great idea to talk about how most of your clients came from word of mouth. Perhaps you could even discuss client events and outings with your client base. You could make the point that your clients are really family instead of mere revenue sources. After you say all that, it will become apparent to even the newest of prospects that word-of-mouth referrals and networking is really a good way for new people to work with you. You could memorize phrases and share them awkwardly. Or you could create a growth mindset, which enable the words phrases to come from your heart.

That's why this book is so important. It not only discusses the mechanics of getting referrals but also will change your mindset so that generating referrals can become much more authentic.

1

Why Referrals Are Important

Research at the University of Connecticut has shown that 89 percent of your clients care more about the relationship than the fees and prices they pay. I'm often asked by clients if they should lower their costs. In fact, sometimes they offer discounts before they even find out a prospect's needs. I read pitches like, "Call me today for a 25 percent discount!"

Unless you are buying something that costs under $100 on the Internet, relationships matter. If you are able to communicate, you will develop rapport and trust that will soon become even more valuable than the fees you're paid.

In research decades ago at the University of California at San Diego, we discovered that trust is worth 17 percent of the gross price of a product or service. Thus, without trust, a competitor could offer a 1 percent discount and steal your client. But with trust, they would have to offer an 18 percent discount for the same outcome. Trust is critical to your profit margin and income.

Forrester Research showed that people buy for three reasons:

1. They want to understand the product or service.
2. They want to know the advisor is in control and watching out for their best interest.
3. They want frequency of contact. They want to hear from you every few months.

If you follow these steps in every client relationship, referrals will come. They are not based on competence or expertise: clients expect competence. Referrals are based on rapport, trust, and frequency of contact. If an attorney does a great job but never communicates again, the client is unlikely to refer. But if the attorney is competent, communicates well during the process, and keeps in touch with you after the service is rendered, your chances of referring business to them goes way up. In fact, that same attorney may never have to spend money advertising again.

Many years ago, one of my coaching clients in Southern California received a referral. The prospect booked an appointment, sat down, and chatted for a few minutes about their mutual friend. Almost on cue, the referred lead started writing a check for $1 million. My client, Tom, said the initial consultation was free. The potential client said he wanted to do business with Tom before he walked in the office. The referral source mentioned such great things that he just wanted to see if Tom could fog up a mirror. This is why referrals are so good. Not only do they open doors, sales are often made before you even make contact.

Why You Don't Ask for Referrals

There are many reasons why we don't ask for referrals. You may have asked often but didn't get any names. Sometimes there could have been awkward silence, which left you feeling rejected or fearing that you would lose the client relationship. Most of the time, it's a combination of these. Including not knowing how to ask.

I remember giving a speech many years ago to the property and casualty insurance company State Farm. At that time, State Farm had the highest agency revenues among all the nonbroker direct writers in the United States. One of the biggest producers told me he had a $20 bill taped to a notice on his desk that said, "If I don't ask you for a referral, take this $20 bill." I asked how many referrals he received during a typical week. He said, "Not many." But he did say many clients walked out the office with $20, hoping the agent would never ask. After $1,000 walked out the door, the agent realized he was losing money and referrals by never asking. While this is a great reminder to build your business, you still have to ask. There are also more elegant ways to do it than by taping a $20 bill to your desk.

The biggest mistake you can make with referrals is failing to ask for them. Often producers avoid this problem by putting the request in an email footnote or in a social media post. One of my clients used a tagline at the bottom of his email saying, "We accept referrals." Another one I love is, "Referrals are the best compliment you can give us." This phrase came from an unsuccessful realtor who had probably heard it at a sales seminar.

Gaining referral relationships is a very personal endeavor. I've spoken around the world for more than forty years, and I've never received a referral impersonally, through an email or text. It's always been through a phone call, in person, or even via webinar.

Matching a verbal referral request with one stated on a business card isn't a bad idea, especially as a reminder, but letting it take the place of a personal request is a big mistake. This is one reason many producers can't seem to build a referral-based business. They think putting the request on a business card or on an office bulletin board will be enough to generate business. It isn't.

Another referral mistake has to do with word of mouth. This means thinking a good job will produce referrals without asking. I frequently ask how my coaching candidates market themselves. They often say, "Word of mouth." Nobody apparently calls their bluff and asks what that means. It's usually a placeholder for, "I don't market myself much, and my business is mediocre." There are some businesses that are truly so unique that prospects beat a path to your door. This could be Airbnb in its first three months, or Zoom during the 2020 Covid-19 crisis. Unless you have a killer unique selling proposition, referrals are critical.

This book assumes that you already believe referrals are useful. In fact, referrals are and will be the best way to gain new business. Referrals are *it*.

Clients always admit that referrals are the ticket to building business. But they also sheepishly admit they come by accident. There probably isn't a week that goes by when I don't hear clients tell me they wish they had more referrals, but they stopped asking years ago.

One of my clients, Andrew, is a financial advisor near Boise, Idaho. He knows how to ask for referrals. In fact, he is really good at it, but he never asks clients for them. I constantly tease him about this. So many clients call every week introducing their friends that Andrew doesn't need to ask. Unless your clients call every week introducing five of their friends, you'd better become proactive.

You Don't Ask Anymore

Many producers at one time had great success in getting referrals but stopped asking. One of my clients, Chris, asks for referrals nearly every time he talks to a client. He averages five to eight new ones weekly. I hope he continues, but at some point in his young career, he will probably stop asking.

Why does this happen? The argument could be made that it works too well. A few years ago, one of my seminar attendees displayed one of my thirty-year-old cassette programs entitled *Peak Performance*. He bragged about using the weekly business development activity program. He even talked about recognizing self-sabotaging fears and his ability to overcome them. He said the year after he bought the audiocassette, his sales doubled. I asked, "Are your sales still increasing?" He said no. He admitted that he stopped using the techniques long ago: the skills he learned worked too well.

This is one of the biggest barriers to building your business with referrals. You will hopefully implement these skills at first. But later you may stop doing them out of laziness, lack of discipline, or even self-sabotage.

Most Referral Generation Techniques Don't Work

Here are some referral generation techniques you are probably familiar with. They don't work. You were taught a faulty system. Predictably, you stopped knocking your head against the wall at some point. A couple of the phrases you were taught are:

1. "I get paid in two ways. First by the business we do. Secondly, by the referrals I get." The client hears that you are unappreciative of the relationship and want more. At least you've remembered to ask. At worst, you have lost rapport and possibly trust in the relationship.

2. "Whom do you know I should be talking to?" This seems like a good way to ask for referrals. But you will rarely get a name, because when you ask, the client immediately tries to remember someone who has previously asked for a provider that does what you do.

I have been an author, speaker, and business coach for forty years. I've never been asked by anyone for the name of a good realtor, financial planner, insurance agent, or attorney. For that matter, I have never even been asked for the name of a good physician. Conversely, I'm regularly asked for the contact information of vendors I talk about. If I brag about my integrative physician, listeners often want a name and telephone number. If I talk about how great my financial planner is, my friends want to know. If I mention success with an attorney, listeners want to know which one.

Advocacy: The Referral Gold Standard

All of this has to do with advocacy—the degree to which your clients talk about you to their friends. Here's a question: what percentage of your clients mention you to their friends? Ninety percent? Eighty percent? How about 50 percent? Research shows that you think that 77 percent of your clients talk about you. The truth is that only 15 percent do. That's right, only 15 percent! We will explore advocacy in detail later, but the Holy Grail in getting referrals is building advocacy. Ironically, the only way to build advocacy is frequency of contact and asking for referrals.

Intimidation: Why We Don't Ask

Another reason we don't ask is intimidation. We are terrified of losing a client. We're afraid that if we ask, they won't think the relationship is valuable: perhaps they will feel offended or will pull back business solely because we asked.

None of this is true. I have never lost a client, nor have any of my clients lost business, because they asked for referrals. Actually, some of my clients have lost business because they failed to follow up on the referrals they received.

The bottom line is the value of the relationship. Are you constantly filling your client's emotional bank account? Are you providing better service than they expect to get? Are you contacting them frequently? Are you earning the right to ask?

Every new coaching client receives training on our three-month phone call script. We train them to catch up on the client's family and update them on new and relevant information. Then they are trained to listen for sales opportunities, but they never pitch. Lastly, they ask for referrals.

The most common pushback my clients get from these phone calls is when they ask for referrals. Clients nearly always say, "I don't know anybody," or, "I will check." My clients hear this response because of they have low balance in their client's emotional bank account. They haven't called in many months, if not years. They haven't earned the right to ask for referrals.

Frequency of Contact, Not Competence

One misconception I hate to hear is that referrals are based on the quality of work. That is actually not true. Clients and prospects expect you to be good. Otherwise they would never have done business with you. But they don't expect a great relationship. If you only appeared competent, your business would never grow.

Clients often don't know the difference between good and great. Many of my clients don't know the difference between spending three hours in preparation for a speech and just walking into the room and wondering what group it is. I am the only one totally aware of the time it takes to prepare. What clients really appreciate during one of my coaching sessions is good content coupled with my focus on listening to their needs, as well as targeting my advice exactly to what they need and want at the time.

Your clients are the same. They expect you to know your products inside and out. As a realtor, they expect you to be aware of the interior and exterior paint colors that will produce offers. If you are a mortgage broker, they assume that you will suggest the best loan available for their needs. But they don't expect that you will keep in contact every couple of months, or that during those calls you will update them on ideas that will make their life better. They don't expect a great relationship, yet the relationship drives advocacy referrals.

Keep in Contact

As I mentioned earlier, 89 percent of your clients care more about the relationship than the price or the fees they pay. Recently I called an insurance company client offering to do a webinar entitled, "How to Thrive in a Crisis." This complimentary webinar would benefit producers and also serve as a great marketing tool for my coaching practice. The day after our conversation, the CEO sent me a referral to another friend who is a CEO with an insurance company. This unsolicited advocacy referral was the result of a relationship, not my skill set. It was because I made contact with a client, not because I'm the best in the world at what I do.

Why Referrals Are Critical

There are five ways to market yourself:

1. **Cold calls.** Although these do develop business, it's a hard slog. Only 4 percent of the people you contact will book any type of appointment. Your eventual closing ratio on these appointments will also be minimal.

2. **Social media.** Neither Facebook, Twitter, nor LinkedIn has a direct response component. Sure, if you buy an ad on Facebook, some people will respond, but not many. Advertisers can expect less than a 0.5 percent response rate at best. Many producers post frequently on Twitter and LinkedIn to build a brand. This branding makes other marketing easier, but posts don't replace relationships. The trick is to get on the phone to find needs.

3. **Direct mail.** Broadcast email advertising will usually net more requests to unsubscribe than qualified responses. Email has actually made snail-mail direct response advertising more effective. Mailboxes full of print ads now have become a trickle.

   What direct mail advertisers always miss is a relationship follow-up. The only way to make direct mail work is by using it to preapproach. Calling a mail recipient a few days after the email or snail mail receipt makes the prospect more receptive. You can usually triple or quadruple response rates by sending direct mail first, followed by a telephone call.

4. **Seminars.** This is by far the most effective way of getting new clients, but it is very expensive. Dinners often cost $50 per person, followed by meeting room expenses and promotional presentation materials. But the real cost lies in direct and email marketing, which can run $2 per recipient. If you are lucky enough to get a 0.1 percent response, the costs are likely to be $6,000 per seminar. If you are lucky enough to do a wonderful seminar, the cost per booked appointment will be $600–

$1,000. With a 25 percent cancellation rate, it could go even higher.

5. **Referrals.** Referrals are free. There are no marketing costs. There is no direct-mail expenditure. There is no food to buy or meeting room to fill. There is no email design cost or lugging letters to the post office. It is simply calling your clients, which they want you to do anyway, then gaining access to their friends, family, and colleagues.

Useful Stats

Marketing can cost anywhere from $400 to several thousand dollars per booked appointment. A new coaching client told me recently that he spends $125 per lead. Often he has trouble connecting and usually leaves a voicemail. His connection ratio is only about 12 percent. His real cost per booked appointment is nearly $1,000. Even with that ratio, he is often the third provider to talk to the purchased lead. I hear these stories constantly. These leads are rarely worth the cost.

Recently one of my clients paid a speaker to deliver a seminar on retirement strategies at a popular restaurant. The presenter, while very good, booked about 35 percent of the room's attendees. This presenter added another $3,000 per seminar to the overall cost. At least my client didn't have to get up in front of the room. Unfortunately, the normal cancellation rate of 25 percent increased to 50 percent when the attendees realized the presenter was not the one attending the appointment. It's amazing what people will do to avoid asking for referrals, the most effective way of building a business known to mankind.

What Is a Client Worth?

Think of the revenue from one client. Let's say your average sales revenue is $1,000. Unless there are more opportunities from that client, that's the only money you will make from that relationship. But let's also say the client gives you three referrals per year, netting a 33 percent closing ratio. Now the relationship from the first client has made you $2,000. But we know from network marketing and the power of compounding interest that your revenue doesn't stop there. Like a virus, each of the clients that were referred will in turn produce more referrals. Let's say that each additional client produces three more referrals per month. The first client netting $1,000 in revenue will quickly morph into hundreds of thousands of dollars—all because you know how to ask for referrals.

Another benefit of referrals is that basing your business on them develops a culture in which referred clients refer you to others. Many years ago one of my clients, Travis, told me that among all the business he received the previous year, 85 percent was from clients who had been referred.

This makes a lot of sense. If a chiropractor has been referred to me, my impression that is that he accepts new patients mainly by referral. If I look online for a local chiropractor, I tend to think that his patients come from online searches. For this reason, you may want to elegantly explain your business model to new clients and customers. Let them know how much you value relationships and that you think of your clients like family.

When I get my haircut at the local Sports Clips, I wait a few minutes for a stylist. I learn their first name, get a haircut, pay, and leave. There is no relationship, no contact after the transaction, and no request for referrals. This means that if I can find a haircut of similar quality, I would leave for a discount.

As I've noted, our research at the University of California at San Diego showed that trust is worth 17 percent of the price of a product or service. That means you can increase your prices by 17 percent without losing clients. But without trust, a 1 percent discount from a competitor will cost you a customer.

When a Client Has a Complaint

I sometimes hear clients say they don't like to keep in contact with difficult clients. Perhaps it was a pricing problem, a paperwork issue, or even a misunderstanding. It is much better to address and solve those issues than ignore them. While this is common sense, it also makes financial sense. The best you can hope for is that one client will talk to three others, developing advocacy. This only works if the relationship is good.

A client with an issue that has been successfully solved brings an advocacy score of twelve to one: this means they will talk to twelve people. One Harvard research study showed that clients are even happier when you have worked hard to solve problems and succeeded. It almost makes you wish for problems to be solved so you can get more referrals. While I understand that some clients will never be happy and will always create conflict, you want to keep and get referrals from those who will refer more if you solve their problems.

How to Get Referrals from Prospects

So far I have written about how to get referrals from existing clients. You can also get referrals from prospects. While it's more difficult, simply asking will support your new referral mindset. If the rapport level is high enough, just asking will get you results.

At the ripe age of twenty-six and new in my career, I received a referral from my first client, Bob Larson, a New York Life Insurance Company manager in Fullerton, California. Bob used me to speak to his thirty agents at a three-hour seminar. Afterward, I asked him for a referral. He gave me the name of Rich Bonadio, an Equitable Life Insurance Company manager twenty miles south in Tustin, California. I was lucky to get an appointment. I gave Rich my sheet of topics. He took a look and pushed it back to me. He said, "I'm not going to book a speaker based on a sheet of paper." As I started to leave, I turned around like the detective Columbo and asked for a referral.

Rich was the president of the General Managers Association in Orange County that year. He gave me a directory of fifty members. I asked Rich if I could mention that we met, and he agreed. I booked ten speeches from that association directory. A referral from a prospect launched my career. Perhaps I could have been successful without the directory. But it was a lot easier—because I asked for a referral from a prospect who kicked me out of his office.

2

Developing a Referral Mindset

I'm often asked about the right way to gain referrals. I usually spend one coaching session on how to ask, then another session on what to say to referred leads in order to book appointments. Another session is required on gaining referrals using social media, followed by two more sessions on getting them from centers of influence. These are experts in a position to refer business to you, like CPAs, attorneys, mortgage brokers, and even realtors. If your career is in one of these industries, you can simply reverse influencers to one of these groups.

Surprisingly, I spend five to eight weeks helping my clients learn the skill sets necessary to gaining and booking appointments from referrals. But that doesn't mean they will change. Most of us will revert back to past behavior. We will go back to what we were doing before. Asking for and getting referrals is much more about having a referral mindset than having a referral skill set. It is much more important to be hungry for referrals than to have the knowledge to ask but never using it.

A referral mindset requires self-discipline, self-confidence, and the ability to change how you think. A few years ago, I worked with a client who wanted to gain more referrals. We worked for weeks and weeks on developing a script that fits his personality and that he was willing to use. I hold my clients accountable to what they commit to. But he failed to implement the skills he had.

Psychologists like me often make good business coaches because when a skill set doesn't work, we are able to look below the surface at psychological problems. This particular client didn't think he had earned the right to ask for referrals. He didn't think he was effective enough for his clients to refer him. He was also afraid of losing his existing business. He was nervous about turning existing clients off. He didn't have the right mindset.

In this chapter, we will explore three mindsets. First, the *fixed mindset* has the potential to sabotage your desire to gain referrals. The *growth mindset* will keep you learning and exploring new techniques. Finally, the *results-focused mindset* will help grow your skills. It will mold your thoughts and behavior toward consistently listening for referral opportunities.

There are three elements of mindset:

1. An emotional component: how people, objects, and events make you feel.
2. A cognitive component that includes your thoughts, beliefs, and expectations.
3. A behavioral component related to how your mindset affects your behavior.

There are three basic stages of mindset:

1. You create beliefs.
2. Your beliefs shape your attitude.
3. Your attitude and beliefs create your mindset.

Think of mindset as the legs under a chair. One leg comprises your beliefs. Another includes your ideas. A third supports your expectations. The fourth leg builds your attitudes. If you take out one leg of the chair, it becomes unstable.

For example, a negative belief would make the referral chair wobbly. An expectation that a client won't give you a referral becomes a self-fulfilling prophecy. If you don't expect referrals, you won't get them. If your expectations are low, you will have a hard time increasing your business.

Discover Your Own Mindset

Even though mindset seems an ephemeral concept, we can measure what your current mindset is and compare it to what you would like it to be. The way you think right now can have an impact on your success later. Let's find out what your current mindset is.

Score these questions on a scale of 1 to 5. If you find yourself in between, feel free to score 2, 3, or 4.

1. *Your IQ is permanent and can't change.*
Until the last decade, psychologists thought you were born with an unchanging IQ. This is defined as the degree to which you can learn. The argument can be made that is easier to learn when you

are young and more difficult as you age. What do you believe? If you agree that IQ does not change, score it as 1. If you believe that IQ does change, give yourself 5.

2. *You worry in the morning.*

It's common to worry in the morning. In fact, the most frequent time for anxiety is when you first wake up. You are concerned about what may happen, and you're thinking about unresolved problems from the past. If you wake up worrying, give yourself a 1. If you don't worry or don't feel anxiety in the morning, give yourself a 5.

3. *You think about protecting yourself emotionally.*

Mindset is also about protecting your emotions. If someone says something inaccurate, do you quickly correct them, or do you joke and make light of the comment? There are many situations where someone slights you. Do you ruminate and fester anger? Or do you ignore these comments? If they unsettle you, score it as a 1. If you ignore deprecatory comments, give yourself a 5.

4. *When things change, you think negatively.*

It's been said that only babies like change. In my book *Why Smart People Make Dumb Mistakes with Their Money*, I discuss *status quo bias*. This is the condition whereby, faced with negative outcomes, people tend to repeat the same behavior. You've heard that insanity is defined as doing the same things over and over while expecting different results. How do you experience change? If it happens, do you immediately think of negative outcomes? If so, then give yourself a 1. If you quickly jump to the opportunities available, give yourself a 5.

5. *When bad things happen, do you blame others?*
One aspect of mindset is how you take criticism and negative outcomes. Do you tend to blame others when things go wrong, or do you look at setbacks as learning experiences? If you blame others, score the question with a 1. If you evaluate setbacks as learning experiences that can make you better, score a 5.

6. *You avoid situations that caused you stress in the past.*
Everybody tries to avoid stress. We stay away from negative people. We avoid situations that have produced stress in the past. We even avoid speaking in front of groups. Public speaking is one of the most stressful situations you could encounter. What do you do? Score 1 if you avoid stressful people or stressful situations. Give yourself a 5 if you look at stressful situations as opportunities, or at least minimize the risk of the engagement.

OK, add your scores up, and let's see how you did.

0–18. If your score falls in this range, your mindset is hurting you. Your thoughts are focused towards a fixed mindset: your intelligence may not grow, bad experiences are to be avoided, and setbacks are unlikely to be viewed as learning experiences.

19–24. There is still some work to do. Although you are not fixed in your mindset, growth is not occurring either. Possibly you have not given up on asking for referrals, but it's a hard slog. With a lack of success, the motivation to ask again has waned.

25–30. If your scores fall in this range, your mindset is helping you. You have a growth focus as well as a tendency to learn. You look at a glass as half full instead of half empty. This is also the beginning of a results-focused mindset, which will set the stage for gaining referrals.

The Fixed Mindset

If your score ranged from 0 to 18, your mindset is likely fixed. Stanford University researcher Carol Dweck says that your attitude toward failure sets the limit on your talents and abilities. She argues that fixed-mindset individuals believe that talent can only take you so far: you certainly can maximize ability, but that's it. In a fixed-mindset world, the most talented people succeed, and the less gifted struggle. In a growth-mindset world, those who work the hardest and learn the fastest can overcome any obstacle.

Fixed-mindset people look at effort simply as a proof of their own talent. Growth-mindset people look at effort as a stepping-stone to the next level. Fixed-mindset people fail partly because of their pessimism.

These mindsets influence the focus and resiliency needed for gaining referrals. You were likely taught in the beginning how to ask for referrals, but the scripts did not work. Not only were they unproductive but you felt embarrassed even asking, so you stopped.

A fixed-mindset producer might agree that referrals are important but is unwilling to ask because requests have never worked in the past. When your referral mindset is fixed, nothing will work because nothing *has* worked.

The growth mindset is the opposite. You may have had the same unproductive training in asking for referrals. Nothing has worked. But unlike the fixed-mindset producer, you are constantly looking for a new script, a new technique—anything that will get you closer.

For example, a webinar is advertised offering to help gain referrals. The fixed-mindset producer won't attend because he has heard it all, done it all, and doesn't believe a webinar will help.

A growth-mindset producer will evaluate the bullet points in the same webinar, hoping for new information, a new way of asking, perhaps even more inspiration.

It's like a child who is thrown into a room of horse manure. The kid immediately screams to be let out. But another child in the same room is laughing and playing. After a while, the researcher walks in and asks why the child is so happy. The growth-mindset child says, "With so much manure, there must be a pony in here someplace."

The growth mindset isn't just a positive outlook. It's not just thinking of the good. It's a way of looking at things that create success. It's a way of motivating yourself to be productive in any situation.

I played pro tennis in the 1970s on the Grand Prix tour. In my youth, not many amateur matches were challenging. I am now a member of the Palisades Tennis Club in Newport Beach, California. The owner, Ken Stuart, also a past pro tour player, once joked that he loves playing with less skilled players, because he is able to work on strokes he is weakest at. What a great attitude! Instead of being disappointed with the lack of challenge, he focuses on developing the part of his game that he rarely gets to practice when pitted against better players.

Growth-mindset people are always looking for a better way of asking for referrals. They are always striving to be more referable. When they hear somebody talk about gaining five referrals in a week, they immediately want to know how the producer asked. They want to learn from every colleague who does it better. Gaining referrals is a mindset. It's a way of thinking. It's possessing the discipline to overcome rejection and sometimes embarrassment while persevering in getting better.

Fixed-mindset people believe:

1. Your IQ is set, and you can't do much to change it.
2. You can learn new skills, but you really can't change your level of talent.

Fixed-mindset people resemble a comment once made by my friend Warren. After playing a mixed doubles match with a weak player, his team lost badly. Warren, a stockbroker with a major firm, is always engaging and funny, but after the loss that day he said, "That's two hours of my life I will never get back." Warren meant it as joke, but it's a common attitude of fixed-mindset people. They view setbacks as a waste of effort instead of stepping-stones to success.

Think about your friends with fixed mindsets. They're likely trying to prove themselves. They probably also try to avoid mistakes. Nobody wants to make mistakes, but a fixed-mindset person won't take the risk.

A good example of a fixed mindset is John McEnroe, the famous tennis player. My professional playing era was 1976 to

1978. McEnroe became famous three years after me in 1981. In his book, *You Can't Be Serious*, John admitted that he never liked tennis. He didn't love to learn, and he didn't thrive on challenges, but he had enormous talent. His natural ability catapulted him to the number one spot in the world for four straight years. If you remember John McEnroe on the court, you also remember his constant tantrums. He would rail, mainly at umpires, although the line judges were also fair game. At times, he was like a blind discus thrower: you never knew where it would land. He would get into confrontations with anybody.

Ivan Lendl was John's toughest competitor in the 1980s. Lendl had a habit of putting sawdust on the grip of his racket to absorb sweat. The ball kids did their best to sweep it off the court. This infuriated McEnroe. Always looking for excuses to deflect from his own mistakes, he would yell at the ball kids, the umpire, and even at Lendl whenever he failed. Losses were somebody else's fault. Poor performance was blamed on others. McEnroe had a fixed mindset.

Imagine yourself in front of a class answering questions from a teacher. You give wrong answers. If you have a fixed mindset, your self-esteem is on the line. Your prestige and image are at risk. Will you be embarrassed? Will your self-confidence take a hit? Will you make excuses? Will you blame the teacher for being unfair?

President George Herbert Walker Bush once vomited on the Japanese prime minister at a state dinner in Tokyo. Even though he had the flu, he attended the dinner; later he apologized profusely. Coincidentally, John McEnroe did the same thing on a Japanese patron hosting him for a tennis match in Tokyo. Immediately after the event, it was the Japanese hostess who apologized profusely. The next day she presented McEnroe with a gift. Because of a fixed mindset, McEnroe said, "That's what it's like to be number one."

How do you cope with your own setbacks? Do you get discouraged? Do you get paralyzed? Or do you look at setbacks with the confidence that you can always recover with enough hard work? With a fixed mindset, setbacks are seen as a sign of a lack of ability. One psychological study showed that if they did poorly on a test, those with a fixed mindset were more likely to say they would study less in the future and consider cheating on the next test. A fixed-mindset person believes that setbacks shine a spotlight on their limitations. With a growth mindset, students who do poorly commit to preparing better for the next test.

You've heard before that when the going gets tough, the tough get going. But this probably applies only to those with a growth mindset.

In another psychological study, students suffering setbacks lost interest and confidence. As the difficulty increased, their commitment and joy decreased. As I mentioned in an earlier chapter, one ten-year-old who was given a puzzle said, "I love a challenge," while another student said, "I'm not good at these." Who do you think performed better?

In short, fixed-mindset people prefer looking good to learning how to be better. They fear effort when it's not guaranteed. They abandon the most effective strategies of hard work when they need it most.

Howard Gardner's book *Extraordinary Minds: Portraits of Four Exceptional Individuals and an Examination of Our Own*

Extraordinariness says that exceptional people have a special talent for discovering their own strengths and weaknesses. Growth-mindset people know what they do well and where they are more challenged. But unlike fixed-mindset people, those with a growth mindset believe they can improve both strengths and weaknesses.

Basketball star Michael Jordan seems like the epitome of someone who was born with great talent and ability. He was destined for greatness. Commercials said, "Be like Mike." He was a demigod in tennis shoes. Nobody would dare say he wasn't special, but he once said, "I'm a person like anyone else." He wasn't special. His great success came because he worked so hard at developing his abilities. He never seemed inherently better than anyone else. In 1978, at fifteen, he was cut by a high-school basketball team. At only five feet ten, he couldn't even dunk a basketball. The fifteen players who made the team had more innate ability. Jordan, possessing a growth mindset, continued to learn, work, and stay committed to being great.

At six feet, I was also cut by my freshman basketball team at age fifteen. But unlike Jordan, I never played basketball again. Too bad that I didn't know about the growth mindset. Luckily, I fell back on tennis and eventually learned how to grow from failure.

In a fixed-mindset world, failure proves the limits of your talents and abilities. In a growth-mindset world, failure is a speed bump, a setback to getting what you want. Getting a bad grade is a setback on your way to getting straight A's. Losing a tennis tournament is a momentary distraction from getting closer to winning the next one.

Sociologist Benjamin Barber once said that he didn't divide the world into success and failure, but into learners and nonlearners. What makes you a nonlearner? One thing is *learned helplessness*. Young children don't quit as they learn to walk. They don't stop talking, even though they babble at first. They just barge ahead. It's only after becoming self-aware that we start to learn that effort is not worth it.

When my daughter Catherine was ten, I enrolled her in an after-school girls' softball team. She was not the best player on the team, or the worst. She constantly complained how bad she was in comparison to other girls. She didn't think she had the talent to be a good player. I kept pointing out how good she was compared to the worst girls on the team. But that was a mistake; I only verified to Catherine that she didn't have the talent to be the best, so she gave up. And I let her. I should have displayed an image of how good she could be with extra effort instead of comparing her to those who were worse off, possibly even encouraging her that she could be better than the best player on the team with enough work.

Fixed-mindset people look at effort simply as proof of their own talent. Growth-mindset people look at effort as a stepping-stone to the next level. The fixed-mindset person fails partly because of pessimism: *I knew that was not going to work! I can't believe I wasted all that time! I could've been doing something else!*

How do you cope with your own setbacks? Do you get discouraged? Do you get paralyzed? Or do you look at setbacks with the confidence that you can recover with enough hard work?

With a fixed mindset, setbacks are seen as an indication of a lack of ability. Hence fixed-mindset people prefer looking good to learning how to be better. They fear effort when it's not guaranteed. They abandon the most effective strategies of hard work when they need it most.

Years ago I watched the movie *Moneyball*. It featured the Oakland Athletics baseball team, run by ex-player Billy Beane (played by Brad Pitt). Beane, by his own admission, was a natural baseball player, but like many pro athletes, he couldn't recover from setbacks. He was coddled by everyone until he got to the pros. He believed that ability, not hard work, would carry him to fame. Luckily, Beane recovered from a fixed mindset and moved to growth. He led the A's from being a losing team to many seasons of record-breaking wins on one of the lowest budgets in baseball.

The team had a statistics guru who calculated each pitcher's probability of success, and matched it with every batter. He also measured each player's likelihood of stealing bases. Some of them ended up scoring more bases and runs than the ones who were statistically better hitters. This is one of the earliest examples of "quant" (statistical) theory in all of sports.

My favorite line in the movie was when Beane told the statistics nerd to fire a player. The quant said, "How I do that?" Beane said, "How do you think you should fire him?" The nerd said, "I think I'll tell him how much we've appreciated him, how much we value him as a player, and how sorry we are to have him leave the team."

Billy Beane then rolled his eyes and said, "If you were going to get killed by gunshot, would you like five in the chest or one in the head?" In the next scene, the nerd simply said to the expendable player, "We traded you to Atlanta. Here's your airplane ticket. I wish you well." To which the player simply said, "OK" and left.

I like this story because we think people are so fragile that they can't take bad news. But I've always believed that being direct is better than dancing around an issue. Trying to spare feelings usually makes things worse in the end.

The Growth Mindset

Stanford psychologist Carol Dweck was very curious about understanding how people cope with failure. She studied children, at first giving them difficult puzzles to solve. One ten-year-old boy pulled up his chair, rubbed his hands together, smacked his lips, and said, "I love a challenge." Another student condescendingly said, "I was hoping this would be a challenge." One student was willing to put in his best effort, while the other dismissed the puzzle as not being worthy of his effort. One was willing to try; the other, not at all. Dweck began to wonder whether human qualities were carved in stone or whether performance could be improved by working harder.

This question of talent versus hard work has troubled psychologists for decades. As a graduate student in the 1970s, I studied nature versus nurture: is behavior based on innate personality or environment? At the time, the belief was that your talents and abilities are set in concrete, and you can make only minor improvements: about 80 percent of who you are, including your abilities and your future success, is baked in, whereas about 20 percent of your potential is what you do with that talent.

We even had ways to measure your potential. One was the IQ (intelligence quotient) test. Today most people think IQ is your unchanging ability to learn. Even modern literature describes IQ as a fixed quantity that cannot be increased. The creator of IQ was Alfred Binet. A French psychologist working in Paris in the early twentieth century, he wanted to identify children who were not profiting from the Paris public school system. He wanted to find kids who would perform better from new educational programs in order to get them back on track.

As a sophomore in high school, I was in a history class I disliked. I toughed it out for a month and then visited my high-school counselor, asking to change. She said all the classes were full except for one, a gifted-student program. She noted that I had already been tested, and my IQ was not high enough to get in.

I told her how much I disliked the class. She finally relented. She gave me a new IQ test with a time limit of three hours. Discouraged, I took the test and reluctantly returned to my boring class. The next day the counselor asked me into her office. She looked shocked. I had scored in the ninety-ninth percentile. She had never seen anyone raise their IQ before. In those days, schools received more grant money when they discovered high-IQ students. The prevailing belief was that they had to be located, not developed. The problem was testing. In those days, IQ was thought to be fixed and never changing; as a result, schools rarely if ever tested twice. The teacher thought I had been mistested earlier instead of believing that anyone could raise their IQ.

IQ also creates self-image. It can determine your goals, your career, and even what you think you have the ability to accomplish. Can you imagine all the kids who have been told their average IQ was not enough to get them into medical, law, or professional school?

Carol Dweck turned that concept upside down. She identified growth-mindset people as those who believe in effort and
focus. This belief can help them achieve goals. Growth-mindset
folks believe better grades come when they try harder. If they are
more careful drivers, they will get into fewer accidents. If they
study harder and take graduate classes, they will advance their
careers. They believe that they can work harder to improve anything in their lives. They also know what they do well and where
they are more challenged, and they believe they can improve both
strengths and weaknesses. Fixed-mindset people believe there's
nothing they can do. Who they are now is all they will be.

Think about someone with a growth mindset. They believe talent and ability can be cultivated. Think about how they confront
setbacks and obstacles. They believe they can get past any obstacle. They look at setbacks as opportunities to stretch themselves. Is
this you? How do you face obstacles? Do you fold, or do you look at
them as challenges that will help you get past the next ones?

One problem with fixed-mindset people is that when they succeed, they may feel superior. They feel their abilities are better than
anyone else's. This feeds into a narrative that is very self-limiting,
because when they fail, their superiority is put at risk. They may
start blaming and making excuses and quit.

Jim Marshall, a former Minnesota Vikings defensive player,
had one of the most embarrassing games of his life against the
San Francisco 49ers. Marshall scooped up a fumble and ran for a
touchdown as the crowd cheered. The problem: he ran the wrong
way and scored for the opposing team. To make matters worse, his
mistake was shown on national television. It was the most devas-

tating game of his life. But possessing a true growth mindset, he thought, "If you make a mistake, you've got to make it right." Then he realized he had a choice: he could sit in misery or do something about it. Focusing on a growth mindset, he played the best football of his career during the second half. The Minnesota Vikings won that game.

We all love to hear these rags-to-riches, failure-to-success stories. But the traits that create these successes can also translate to your life. With a growth mindset, you can learn to succeed. With a fixed mindset, you are caught in your own failure.

The Results-Focused Mindset

When I was in graduate school, an intense area of study was cognitive psychology. A metaphor given to help us learn better was how computer code is written. Each instruction is created with a result in mind. The final computer program is the creation of thousands of lines, which make a computer work. Mindset works the same way. Your mindset comprises millions of lines of code you have created over the years. It produces behavior that in turn creates the results you experience. Performed often enough, these turn into habits.

You're probably reading this book because you want to improve your results by changing to a more constructive, outward, growth-focused mindset. I have to admit that I've really never believed people can change. During seminars, I usually spend at least twenty minutes talking about the fact that people are static. Of the Americans married this year, 62 percent will be divorced in ten years. How about second marriages? Do you think the percentage is higher or lower? Yes, it's much higher. The divorce rate for second marriages within ten years is 78 percent. During seminars I jokingly say, "The reason it's so high is because you took yourself with you to the second marriage!" Are you wondering about third marriages? This time around, divorce rates decrease to 36 percent within ten years. It's probably because people realize they've messed up the first two marriages, so they'll work hard to avoid failing with the third.

The rate of prison recidivism is 83 percent within five years after getting out of jail. I don't think it's because the food is so good and the sports are so much fun that convicts can't wait to get back. I think it's because people have a very difficult time changing.

The great developmental psychologist Jean Piaget once said that personality—including your personality, values, ethics, and even how you think—is created and completed between two and seven years old. But don't be discouraged. Although I believe that people have an enormously difficult time changing their mindsets, they can. And the harder you work on applying what you learn, the more you'll be able to improve and develop a better mindset.

The attitude that combines both the outward and growth-oriented aspects of mindset and will serve you best is the results-focused model. Becoming outward-minded and knowing how your decisions will affect others is important. You can't maintain a healthy, productive mindset without considering others. At the same time, a growth-focused mindset will maintain your motivation and enable you to believe that anything is possible as long as you work hard enough. It will help you create optimism and remind you that your genes and innate talent account for only a very small part of success.

The results-focused mindset will enable you to keep an end result in mind. It will also help you stay positive when setbacks occur, maintaining your motivation in spite of discouragement. The results-focused mindset doesn't merely help you learn from mistakes, as the growth mindset does: it helps you apply those lessons toward a goal.

Years ago, I spoke at a road show in the financial services industry in Manchester, New Hampshire. I had a partnership with the company sponsoring the seminar. I asked the wholesaler if one of my local clients could attend, but the guest was a competitor and inappropriately tried to recruit the attendee he sat next to. It wasn't until the next month at another seminar in Boston that I heard about the infraction. The wholesaler accused me of setting my guest up to steal her business. It was an outrageous accusation, since I was doing more than fifty seminars a year for this company. Why would I jeopardize that relationship? But she didn't back down, and I saw only futility in protesting my innocence. I asked what I could do to rebuild trust. We decided that I would waive my speaking fee for my upcoming speech in Boston. I asked if that could be the end of the incident. She agreed.

A month later, another wholesaler from the same company called me from Chicago and canceled three speeches with me. The Boston wholesaler, on a nationwide company conference call, had accused me of sabotaging her business. This was the wholesaler for whom I waived my speaking fee and who said the issue was resolved.

The deceit was obvious. The infraction was deleterious. With a fixed mindset, only blame would make me feel better. With a growth mindset, I could overcome it if I just worked harder. But with a results-focused mindset, the setback spurred me to be more creative in bypassing this company, even though it had given me so much business. I discovered a new direction for hitting my goals that year. Since then, I have learned never to depend on one company, or a single industry, for so much business. I have also learned to be more careful when allowing guests to attend, and I am more sensitive to any conflicts they may bring.

All of us have stories of being wronged or slighted. But with a results-focused mindset, we can use those lessons to achieve our goals more effectively. All of us can learn to be more productive. How do you succeed? By gaining wisdom. How do you gain wisdom? By learning.

Recasting Your Mindset

One technique you can use to develop a results-focused mindset is called *recasting*. As I've written in my books *Willpower: The Secrets of Self Discipline* and *Mastering Self-Confidence with NLP*, there are very specific things you can do today to create a more effective mindset.

Recasting works much like a frame around a picture. A poor frame can make any painting look worse, just as a beautiful frame can make even a mediocre painting look substantially better. In some cases, the frame can look better than the picture itself.

Recasting is built on the concept that there are no good or bad events in your life, only your perception. One of my favorite stories about one's perception of results is from the movie *Charlie Wilson's War*. The story is about how jaded congressman Charlie Wilson (played by Tom Hanks) was able to help the Afghan mujahedeen warriors defeat the Soviets in the 1980s, during the Reagan administration. (This also led to the start of the Al-Qaeda terrorist movement, but that is another story.)

A CIA officer, played by the late Philip Seymour Hoffman, cautions Wilson not to be too sure they have done something glorious. To make the point, he told the story of a Zen master who observes the people of his village celebrating a young boy's new horse as a wonderful gift. "We'll see," the Zen master says. When the boy falls off the horse and breaks a leg, everyone says the horse is a curse. "We'll see," says the master. Then war breaks out, the boy cannot be conscripted because of his injury, and everyone now says the horse was a fortunate gift. "We'll see," the master says again. The moral of our story is that you can recast your perception of outcomes. You can change your mindset. You can change your results.

Recasting is not exactly visualization. It is more a rethinking or restructuring of how you think about a concept or idea. For example, if you decide to go into work at 7 a.m., your first inclination might be to think, "If I go in that early, I will feel tired." To recast that idea, you might think, "If I go into work at 7 a.m., I will be able to get an extra two hours of work done without interruption. This in turn will help me achieve my goals more effectively."

I once developed a friendship with an airline pilot. His emotional picture frame was his flying career. He connected everything to flying or something related to it. If he saw a news report about

Paris, he'd talk about a recent trip there. If we discussed food, he'd bring up airline cuisine.

Most people don't structure their thoughts to that extent, but we all see life in a way that either limits or empowers us. While my friend saw his experiences through the filter of aviation, it certainly served his objective of being a successful pilot. The way he framed the world made even the drudgery of his work enjoyable, because he saw the entire world as if it were related to flying.

You can use recasting to develop a results-focused mindset. The key to recasting is to associate positive experiences with your goals and objectives and to disregard the obstacles, or at least to see them as opportunities to learn and cope. If you can do this, you'll have much more control over your life.

Context and Content Recasting

Two types of recasting that will change your attitude away from the negative to the positive aspects of a new mindset are *context* and *content recasting*.

CONTEXT RECASTING

Context recasting refers to your ability to take a negative situation and make it positive in another context. For example, say your flight is delayed four hours because of weather. You could become irritated, as most passengers would be, or you could get four hours of work done without interruption. With a fixed mindset, you would curse the airline. With a results-focused mindset, you would relish the chance to use the extra time constructively.

I was recently stuck in the Newark airport, which has the highest number of delays in America. Passengers were irate when a United Airlines flight was canceled. Instead of becoming angry, I picked out a chair next to a power plug and started to work on this book. I was actually pretty happy that I had time to get some work done. (A recent news report showed that only 15 percent of travelers take advantage of travel as an opportunity to work or get things done. Most sleep or simply stare into space.)

I have written eight books while flying on airplanes. I could not have accomplished that if all my flights had been on time, or if I hadn't taken advantage of the extra time that became available.

Even so, recasting is more than making lemons into lemonade. At one time the 3M Corporation had trouble with the durability of one of its adhesives. The company's goal was to sell more of it, but the defect made for dwindling sales. Although the adhesive was not effective at bonding materials permanently, it did bond them temporarily. One researcher used recasting and put just a little bit of the adhesive on the back of a piece of paper to make it stick to nearly any surface. Was there an application for which this adhesive could be used? You guessed it—Post-it Notes were born.

Here is another example of a context recast: There once was a farmer who owned an old mule. The mule fell into the farmer's well. The farmer heard the mule braying, but after assessing the situation, he decided that neither the mule nor the well was worth the trouble of saving. Instead he called his neighbors together, told them what had happened, and enlisted them to help haul dirt to bury the old mule in the well, putting him out of his misery.

Initially, the old mule was hysterical. But as the farmer and his neighbors continued shoveling and the dirt hit the mule's back, it suddenly dawned on him that every time a shovel load of dirt landed on his back, he would shake it off and step up. This he did over and over again. Shake it off and step up . . . Shake it off and step up . . . Shake it off and step up . . .

No matter how distressing the situation seemed, the old mule fought panic and just kept right on shaking it off and stepping up.

It wasn't long before the old mule, battered and exhausted, stepped triumphantly over the wall of that well. What seemed that it would bury him had actually blessed him—all because of the manner in which he handled his adversity.

CONTENT RECASTING

The second type of recasting, *content recasting*, is the mental act of changing what an event means to you. For example, a Christian looks at death not as the end of life but as a new beginning in the kingdom of heaven.

For a more down-to-earth example, take an entrepreneur who recently went bankrupt selling commodities in Chicago. He now has a successful business that consists of several busy hot-dog shops. He describes his first business failure as getting an intense education in running a business.

Think of a project you've been putting off, like repairing a piece of furniture. You can choose to see the job as taking away from the time you'd otherwise spend watching sports on TV, or you can choose to see yourself working on the repair, listening to the game on the radio, and enjoying the experience more than you would had you actually been watching TV.

This technique works. You simply have to change the negative image of working on the furniture to one where you're having fun. You can even recast an image to include your whole family helping and telling jokes. If you do this, your attitude toward the dreaded experience *will* change.

If this technique seems unbelievably simplistic, think of the last time you did the gardening or another household chore you'd been putting off. Didn't you avoid it for a long time, only to feel after you'd done it that the experience wasn't so bad after all?

My friend, sports commentator Terry Bradshaw, tried his hand as a motivational speaker. He took what he learned from the field and the speaking stage to the TV sports desk. He recast his attitude and image in a way that empowered him to achieve his goals. He knew he wasn't as articulate as basketball great John Wooden, nor did he have the speaking flair of my client, Minnesota NFL Hall of Fame quarterback Fran Tarkenton, or even the attention to detail of former Washington Redskins quarterback Joe Theisman, but he did have a huge amount of enthusiasm. He worked on developing a flair for enthusiastic delivery in a way that every audience would find contagious.

The difference between recasting and merely being positive is the permanence of the new thought. If you replace old negative memories with new, positive perspectives, you will be able to keep past events from limiting your future success. This in turn will help you change your mindset.

Recasting Emotions, Behaviors, and Memories

It is even possible to recast emotions, behaviors, and memories. This technique is based on understanding neurolinguistic programming (NLP), developed by researchers John Grinder and Richard Bandler. The theory goes that your unconscious controls how you experience and perceive both past memories and current events. It consequently controls all sorts of habitual behaviors, which frees you to think about more important and urgent things. For instance, you don't consciously think about braking your car when you come to a stop sign, but you brake nonetheless. That you do so unconsciously frees you to think consciously about the scenery, people, or conversations around you.

However, such unconscious habits may not always be good for you. In some cases, such as when you try to diet, your mindset may turn inward and become negative.

A couple of years ago, I spoke to a woman who had enormous trouble losing weight. She had tried every diet she could think of, and still nothing worked. After several conversations, I learned she had been raped as a teenager. She still struggled with that memory, as well as with the low self-esteem she'd had ever since. She was attractive, but her poor self-image was hard to alter after twenty-five years. Because of this low self-esteem, she found it impossible to lose weight. The extra weight simply confirmed her poor self-image. Being thin violated how she saw herself, so she was unable to lose the weight.

Like this woman, we need to find ways to influence our unconscious to get it to support our goals. To do this, we first need to know how we process information.

NLP holds that people basically perceive the world in one of three different ways: in pictures, sounds, or feelings.

Picture people make sense of the world by constructing or recalling images in their minds. If they can't make a mental picture of what you're saying, they may have trouble getting a clear understanding of your ideas.

Sound people make sense of what they hear based on how things sound and react accordingly. They often talk to themselves in order to understand a message.

Feeling people tend to react viscerally. They get a gut emotion while talking to you. They may feel hot or cold about you or an idea after just a few minutes of interaction. Many people call this *intuition.*

If you knew what system you use to perceive the world, could you change your mindset? You bet. The following approach focuses on your unconscious thought mode to help you recast your emotions, behaviors, and memories so they are more supportive of a results-focused mindset.

Here is the four-step approach to recasting emotions, behaviors, and memories. If you use these steps, you will improve your mindset.

1. **Identify the pattern of behavior or thought you would like to change.** For example, athletes often think in visual terms. Many of my tennis buddies tell me they pick a place on the court to serve to. Then they visualize the spot in their minds as they hit the ball.

If you want to hit a serve differently, you might imagine the spin the ball after it leaves the racket instead of focusing on the mechanics of holding the racket. One way to use visualization is for a slice serve in tennis (that is, a hit with sidespin). You might imagine the racket glancing off the side of the ball. You could picture the tennis ball being peeled like an orange by your racket. You might also imagine the ball jumping straight up as it lands on the other side of the court. This would give you a very powerful mental image in tennis. But it is also an example of how to use visualization in any other task you want to accomplish.

In 1977, I was struggling while playing a professional tournament in Linz, Austria. I had only competed on clay courts for a few months, and still had trouble moving on this unstable surface. My serves didn't have the same kick and speed as on the hard courts I was used to. The clay surface caught the ball and slowed it down. The harder I tried to hit the ball, the more mistakes I made. I lost five games in a row and became desperate.

I had just finished a book by Tim Gallwey entitled *The Inner Game of Tennis*. Gallwey was the Zen master of tennis. His teaching method—really NLP before there was NLP—was to focus, not on how you hit the ball, but on the result. This technique was totally different from any teaching method up to that time. I was desperate and ready for anything. After all, if I kept making the same mistakes, I would lose the match.

I picked out a pebble on the clay surface where I wanted my serve to land, and just let it rip. My ball landed within inches of the target and aced the German national champion, who was my opponent that day. My next serve was a slice and kicked so high that it caught my opponent totally off guard.

The result: my service game immediately improved, and I won the match. This happened because I concentrated more on the result and the goal than on the method to reach them. Methods are always important, but sometimes we get so stuck in technique and process that we paralyze ourselves.

2. **Use signals from your unconscious to determine the background reason for your unwanted behavior and to help change a habit pattern.** (Most of our habitual behaviors and thoughts are unconscious anyway.) The way to go about this is to make your mind go blank and then pose a question to which you are looking for a "yes" or "no" answer. Separate the difference between the background reason for the behavior from the behavior itself. Again, do this by using unconscious signals that can be answered with "yes" and "no" questions.

Identify a new, desirable behavior that is more in line with your goals. Use your unconscious to help, using "yes" and "no" questions as a guideline.

Determine whether the new behavior fits in with who you are without inner conflict. Again, use "yes" and "no" questions as guidelines.

For example, say the woman in our previous example continued to try to lose weight, but her unconscious didn't support this goal. Using step one, she would identify her eating habits as the behavior she wanted to change. Being thinner would be the goal to which she was consciously committed.

The next step in this process would be to get a signal from her unconscious about this goal. Again, the key to tapping into your unconscious is to think of questions with "yes" or "no" answers. Then clear your mind and pose these questions to your unconscious. The answers, negative or positive, won't come in words. They will be more of an image or feeling, or even what you hear yourself thinking. This is because some of the most common signals our unconscious sends us are based on our dominant thought mode. If your most powerful mode is using pictures, for example, be passively aware of signals like images in your mind. Are those images dark, light, or small? Your unconscious may signal you by changing those images. It may make an image smaller, signaling "no," or brighter, signaling "yes." Some people will even see a flashing "yes" in the mental picture as a response to a question.

If you want to lose weight, can you picture yourself as thin? Is the image pleasing? Is the image of a thin body bright and big, or dim and small? If it's dim and small, your unconscious may not be supportive of your weight loss program.

If your dominant mode is auditory, be aware of noises like ringing or other sounds that become louder or quieter when there is opposition. Can you hear people telling you how thin you look? Or do you hear ridicule because you're too thin?

If your most powerful mode is feeling, watch for physical sensations. You might become aware that your fingers are tingling, or your legs might get warmer in response to the questions you ask. You also might get a feeling in your gut. Do you feel warmly excited about being thin, or do you feel dread as you contemplate the work it will take to lose weight? All of these signals are common, but you may feel others as well. Just remain aware of any signals your unconscious wants to use as you ask for "yes" or "no" answers to questions.

You might be thinking how silly it is to pay attention to your dominant thought mode as you evaluate your goals, but you do this all the time. You get a feeling before you buy something. You hear a voice in your head that something may not be right. You visualize problems or get excited about future opportunities. With the technique I'm describing, we are just using NLP to tap into the processes you are already using.

Tapping into your unconscious is essential for determining the background reason for any unwanted behavior. Ask your questions and then be alert for answers that come from your dominant mode of reacting. The woman who wanted to lose weight discovered there was a secondary gain to being overweight—diminished attention from men. By asking herself questions, she determined that her unconscious resisted losing weight because being heavy saved her from the pressure of dating.

To get your unconscious to stop protecting you through this secondary behavior, you need to acknowledge what it has been doing. Then you need to ask if there are other ways to protect yourself from the perceived threat besides the undesired behavior. Again, use a series of "yes" and "no" questions to learn what these alternatives might be.

In the case of the overweight woman, she might have asked her unconscious if she could protect herself from the pressures of dating by deciding not to go out with anyone for a certain period of time. She could also have asked was whether dating was really all that threatening.

You see how it goes. Asking these questions occurs in a sort of stream of consciousness, in which one question leads to another.

Keep in mind, though, that from time to time all of us see secondary gains in not changing our mindset. My tardiness in practicing the trumpet at age twelve grew out of my dislike of the instrument. I was consequently late to lessons and procrastinated practicing, but I was never late to baseball or tennis practice.

Likewise, procrastination about going back to college may lie in an unconscious desire not to leave your job as a waitress or bartender. Maybe you really like this job, even though you don't make enough money. The truth is, you don't procrastinate doing the things you love. If you think you want the goal but still procrastinate, you need to get your unconscious involved to find out why.

I once read a report about a pro golfer who, ten years earlier, had been ranked in the top twenty in the world. He hadn't won a tournament in these ten intervening years and thought he had the "yips," a tendency to hit the ball with a jerk instead of a smooth, controlled swing. It's like trying to be extra careful around expensive china and then nervously breaking it all.

The interviewer asked some probing questions about the pro's family and discovered that his spouse wasn't especially supportive. She wanted him to take a job as a local country club pro. He felt guilty about all the travel time away from his family and had trouble committing to his demanding goal enough to get back into the top twenty.

3. **Create a new behavior in line with your goals.** Again, let's use the example of the woman who wanted to lose weight. Through

her unconscious, she found that she had a secondary gain from doing just the opposite (it saved her from the pressure of dating). A solution for her was to change her goal of how much weight she would lose—say ten pounds instead of twenty-five. This way her behavior still changed, her goals were still met, and her unconscious had time to adjust. Thus she would be more readily able to support a further weight loss in the future if she so desired.

4. **Make sure the new behavior is in line with your unconscious goals.** The woman who wanted to lose weight tried to get a sense of her new self-confidence in the context of, "Is this really what I want, consciously and unconsciously?" As she checked her unconscious by using "yes" and "no" questions, she also made a commitment to uncover new ways and techniques to take the weight off and keep it off. She then used the unconscious signals she had previously accessed to get her unconscious to embrace her goal of losing weight. Once she had done all these things, she was ready to work toward achieving her objective, albeit a little at a time.

When you use visualization and recasting, self-confidence can be like Aladdin's lamp—it can grant you just about anything you wish for. All you have to do is know how to rub the lamp. As the old saying goes, beware what you wish for. You may get it!

3

How to Ask for Referrals

As I've written earlier, you have been taught to ask for referrals in a very manipulative way. Most sales pros ask for referrals as if the client is expected to produce them. The mistakes range from "Don't keep me a secret" to "I get paid in two ways."

A craftier way of asking is: "Whom should I be talking to?"

The biggest foible nearly everybody falls into is asking whom the client knows. When they hear this request, clients automatically struggle to remember which of their friends requested someone with your skill set. Since they can't remember, they say, "I don't know anybody." Your clients have a memory of about three days at best. Even if someone asks for someone like you, they probably forgot the name and even when the request occurred.

I've been a speaker and author for more than forty years. I can count on one hand the number of people who have asked for expert referrals. One asked for the names of great speakers they could use in the future. One asked me for a CPA. But that's it. Three requests for expert referrals in forty years! It's no wonder your clients say, "I don't know anybody." No one asked them for a person like you in the last few days that they can remember. Your requests don't work because the question for your client is for someone who never asked and isn't remembered.

The Three-Month Phone Call

There is an answer to gaining frequent referrals on a consistent basis. The solution is the *three-month phone call*. According to Forrester Research, people want three things from you, especially when the expenditure requires advice and expertise in making a purchase. These three needs are:

1. **What am I buying?** Can I understand this functionally?
2. **Is my advisor watching out for me?** Are they thinking about my needs first?
3. **Is there frequency of contact?** Do I hear from them during and after the transaction? To prove this, the next time you ask somebody to buy, let them know first that the purchase will be the last time you will ever speak to them. Then listen for any objections. My guess is, they will never do business with you. There is an implicit contract suggesting the buyer expects a relationship after a transaction. The more expensive the purchase, the more likely the buyer are to expect a relationship.

In 2015, I bought a new Porsche Cayenne from a dealer in Long Beach, California. I got along with David, the salesman, very well. He went out of his way to answer my questions and walk me through the process. I was very impressed. The Cayenne was a dealer demo that had been on the lot for six months. I was ecstatic with the purchase and couldn't believe the great deal.

About a month later, I called David with a question about the warranty. I reached his voicemail and got a call back from one of the administrative people at the dealership, who answered my question. But then I asked David to call me back. He never did. He delegated the relationship to somebody else. He had devalued me to being merely a transaction. Even though I love my purchase, David will never get referrals from me in the future. Either he is too successful selling $100,000 vehicles, or he doesn't know what it takes to keep a customer.

What should he have done? Keep in contact. This is always the answer.

The de facto frequency of contact with a client is three months. Any more and the client is likely to forget you. If you call more frequently, the client may feel inundated. This three-month concept has gelled through forty years of asking clients how often they would like to hear from me. The responses range from two months to six, but never more than that.

I'm often asked about newsletters and email broadcasts. Can those take the place of a phone call? I frequently ask my coaching clients how often they contact their own clients. They usually say monthly, but that contact is usually in the form of a monthly newsletter. Surprisingly, they think a newsletter can take the place of an engaged contact relationship. Social media, newsletters, videos, and any other mass-market tools are good branding, but they are poor tools for building relationships. Nobody is going to respond to a newsletter asking them to purchase a major service or product without first wanting to engage in a conversation.

The following is a script on how to ask for referrals. It's called the *three-month call script*. The whole call should last about fifteen minutes.

1. **Catch up.** The three-month call script can be done on the phone or face-to-face. This step reminds them of the last conversation and asks, "What's new? When I last spoke to you, you had a new granddaughter. How is she doing?" This will allow you to reestablish rapport. Gaining trust here is critical to the rest of the conversation. This first part, catching up on whatever happened since the last conversation, may take the bulk of the time on the call.

2. **Update.** This part of the call will keep both clients and prospects interested in hearing from you. Most people never call clients and customers. The ones that do often don't go past "What's new?" It doesn't take long before the client becomes bored with these calls.

A few years ago, my air conditioning system broke down. The HVAC vendor offered a discount if I would pay a $100 annual fee for quarterly service. It started as a good deal. The telemarketer called after three months, asking if my system was working well. I told them there were no problems. They offered to send a technician to make sure. I told them again everything was OK, and I didn't need a visit. Three months later, the same conversation occurred, and I again told them not to come. By the time of the next call three months later, I just didn't answer.

This is what happens if all you do is call to catch up on what's new. You have to offer new information or an update that is useful and that the client or customer wants to hear. Here are a couple of examples of an update:

REALTOR

Give your client an update on real estate prices and/or mortgage rates. Give them an update on houses in their neighborhood that have just sold. These comps will be of great interest to your homeowner.

FINANCIAL ADVISOR

Give your client an economic or market update. Let them know about interest rates or tax law changes. You can even tell them what the market has done and what it may do in the next six months—anything that your client may be interested in.

AUTO SALES

People who buy cars are interested in changes and updates to their brand. A BMW owner is probably interested in new models for the next year, even in features of their current car they weren't aware of.

I was a BMW guy until 2004. Ready for a new model, my wife saw a used Porsche 911 turbo in the back lot of a dealership in Irvine, California. She asked if I'd ever driven a Porsche. I was very curious. I took the speedster out for a test drive on the freeway and flew below radar. I was hooked that day and continue to be. I ordered a new 911 from Germany. After eighteen months, I lost my patience and bought a 911 Cabriolet in 2006 from a dealer in Pasadena, California. Within the next three months, I drove with my wife up Highway 1 to Monterey. We even made the four-hour drive to Las Vegas from Santa Ana. I read magazine after magazine about Porsche 911 features. Since the salesman didn't know what you now know, he made the transaction and never kept in touch. I would have loved to have heard from him. Apparently car sales producers have too much business.

Fast-forward a couple of years. A local realtor with Berkshire-Hathaway in Orange County, California, made an even worse mistake. Corine came over for a home appraisal. She asked what it would take to list my house. I first asked about her marketing strategy to gain new clients. She did everything: door knocks, scratch pads on door steps, advertisements, and even a monthly newsletter. I told her about the three-month phone call. People buy houses every seven years and refinance every 3.5 years. Getting a new buyer and seller is as simple as being in contact at the right time.

Corine called me twice in six months. Even though I told her all about the update process, she either forgot or chose not to listen. On the first call she said, "I just called to find out how you are. How is the family? How are the kids? Do you want to list your house yet?"

I again told her exactly what to say on the update: I wanted to hear about whether my house went up or down in value. I wanted to hear about where mortgage rates were headed. I wanted to hear about anything happening in the next year that could affect my home's value. She understood and was very pleasant, but when she called again three months later, she made the same mistake. She forgot the update and only asked about my family and when I would list my house. I gave up and didn't answer the telephone again.

All you have to do is be prepared to update your client or customer with new ideas and information they can use. If you are a contractor, you could let a homeowner know about a new project. If you run an IT consulting company, it can be a new software application. I think you get the idea.

3. **Bridge and referral.** The update is really just to get the conversation started. We are only trying to get the client or prospect to talk. At this point, we need to find needs.

The way to find needs is called the *five bridge*. This is a way to sell without selling and close without closing. You are simply "listening" people into buying from you. Research from US Trust discovered that only 6 percent of all purchases occurred because clients were made to understand; 86 percent bought because they felt understood. The more you can help a prospect, client, or customer feel listened to, the higher your closing ratio.

The Five Bridge

1. **Introductory sentence.** The first step is to get them to talk. Then you can listen for needs. The more you talk, the fewer needs you will discover. This is not a time to pitch. It's a time to listen. After you give an update, ask how they feel, not what they think. We don't want them to spout off what they heard on the news. We want to know how it all affects them. How do they feel?

If you are a financial planner and update the economy and the stock market, find out their feelings, not their CNBC talking points. We want to hear how volatility is making them worry. We don't want to hear what Jim Cramer said last week.

If you are a realtor, you also want to ask how the client feels. You don't want to hear about their economic predictions. You want to know how they feel about their home value and what their plans are for the future. Perhaps they want to remodel. Maybe they want to add a second story. Perhaps they want to ask how much a construction project will increase their home value. You can direct the conversation to what the client wants to build and perhaps how to save costs. Maybe you could steer the conversation toward avoiding the headache of construction by moving into a house better suited to their needs. You could focus the conversation in any direction. All you have to do is listen.

2. **Search for needs (and get three).** Life Insurance Marketing Research Association (LIMRA) research has discovered that if you can uncover one need, a sale occurs 36 percent of the time. If you can uncover two needs, 56 percent will buy from you. If you can uncover three needs, a sale will occur 92 percent of the time. This means you have to listen. You can't pitch or sell.

You're going to be very tempted to tell people what to do. You will be very motivated to talk about a new annuity, a new house you just listed, or a new mortgage product. Don't be tempted. You need to stop talking and just listen. Show empathy. Bite your tongue. Anything you say will work against you. If you talk about a solution, your client will not feel understood.

They will only think you're trying to pitch something. Don't sell. Just listen.

Sometimes a client or prospect will not be as talkative as you would like. Sometimes you have to present problems and ask if they have solutions. This is called "hurt and rescue." Hurt and rescue means that you have identified a concern and want to know if it also concerns them.

For example: "I was thinking about you last week regarding your retirement over the next ten years. My concern is that if you have a long-term illness, it could be financially devastating for your family. There is a 70 percent chance that will happen before you pass away. What have you done so far to find a solution to this concern?"

Here's another example: "Mortgage rates over the next year are predicted to rise 1 percent. Your adjustable loan will be impacted. What plans have you made to try to prevent a $300 increase in your mortgage payments?"

Both of these are good examples of hurt and rescue. You are presenting a problem and asking if they have any solutions. If they push back and say they are not concerned, be prepared with backup statistics. For example, long-term care costs are $6,000 to $8,000 per month for an average of six months. If you are a Porsche salesperson and know your customer wants a new car in the next couple of years, you might say "The new model is predicted to be $15,000 more than last year's. I know that you want a new car; what are your plans to mitigate any price increases?" After they say they have no plans, ask, "Does that concern you?" Perhaps they will say they will buy a used car. Your hurt and rescue response could be,

"That is a great idea, but you have always wanted a new car. What are you plans to avoid the price increase?"

3. **Recap.** The recap is God's gift to sales. If done right, it makes you listen. As I mentioned before, only 4 percent buy because they understand; 86 percent buy because they feel understood. The more you make prospects or clients feel understood, the higher your closing ratio and sales.

The way to do that is to recap your listener's statements. As they talk about three needs, you write them down. You restate their comments back to make them feel understood. For example, "If I heard you correctly, you said you wanted to decrease volatility, lower taxes, and avoid running out of money during retirement. Did I get that right?" Or you could say, "If I heard you correctly, you want a car with no more than five thousand miles, still with a warranty, and no more than a year old. Did I hear you correctly?"

Both of these statements will make your prospect or client feel understood.

A few years ago, I was sick in bed with the flu. Flipping for something to watch on TV, I came across a program on Showtime called *The Affair*. It was about a husband who had an affair with a waitress. During the fifth season, the husband was divorced, and the waitress was married to someone else. The ex-wife married a neurologist and moved to Malibu, California. In the psychotherapist's office, the ex-wife said, "I hate it here. I really miss New York City. I can't stand the blue skies every day. The ocean is too boring. I miss the seasons like in New York."

The psychotherapist said, "If I heard you correctly, you can't stand the blue skies. The ocean is really boring, and you miss the seasons in New York City. Did I get that right?" The wife said, "Yes, that's exactly how I feel. I miss New York City."

This is exactly why I became a business psychologist and not a clinician. I would have said to this client, "Stop wasting my time and get a life. The weather is awesome, and the views are spectacular. Why can't you just be happy with what you have?" You would never want a psychotherapist like me! I am too direct, with too little empathy. Still, the therapist's response here is a good example of recapping.

If you really want to make people feel understood, recap what they say. If you want to have a great marriage, recap your spouse's comments. If you want to have better friendships, recap your buddies' opinions, except when you teasingly call them out on how stupid their opinions are (the way my friends do). It's almost impossible to have a heated discussion with people who listen to and acknowledge your opinions. It's also nearly impossible for a prospect to reject you if they feel understood.

4. **Trial close.** Trial closing is another gift from God. It is a way to get people to commit to a solution and move to the next step. A trial close is the process of repeating three needs and asking if they want to find a solution. For example, "If we could take a look at a one-year-old car with less than five thousand miles along with a warranty, would that be helpful?" Another example: "If we could look at a financial plan that would avoid volatility, ensure that you will never run out of money, and lower taxes,

would that be the right way to go?" These are just two examples of not only making people feel understood but also committing them to doing something about it.

My goal is to make sure you never experience rejection ever again. Nobody should ever say no to you. Nobody should ever stall you or tell you they want to think about it. From now on, recap and trial-close with anybody you're trying to do business with. This works in any situation. From now on, the only time you will get rejected is if you forget to use the steps.

After a pro tennis career of only two years, I still play four times a week. I'm slower on the court now, with a much less powerful serve than when I played in the 1970s, but I can still compete with twenty- and thirty-somethings. A few years ago, after a doubles match, four of us went up to the bar at the Palisades Tennis Club in Newport Beach, California. One of my buddies said, "So you're a business psychologist, right?"

I said, "That's what I do."

He then went on a diatribe about how much he disliked one of his salespeople. He said, "I have this idiot sales guy who comes in late, leaves early, annoys my staff, and isn't even hitting his numbers."

I knew exactly what to say. I couldn't wait to spout advice on how to handle his producer. I wanted to talk about the three-step praise, three-step reprimand, and even the critical path method of probation and performance improvement. This is a skill set for leading people after you first hire and what to do before you fire them.

Instead I used our recap and trial-close technique. I recapped by saying, "Let me get this straight. He comes in late, leaves early, annoys your staff, and isn't even hitting his numbers. Did I get that right?"

He said, "Absolutely! I can't stand this guy."

I then trial-closed by saying, "If we could take a look at what to do with this guy, would that be helpful?"

My tennis buddy looked at his beer for a few seconds and said, "Nope. I've got it covered."

What if I had given my friend free advice? After all, he asked for it, didn't he? If I did let him know my thoughts, he would have rejected them. He didn't want to find a solution. He didn't want to know what to do. In this case, all my friend wanted to do was vent. He only wanted me to listen.

Even so, with your clients and prospects, listen for three needs, recap what they say, and trial-close. If you use these steps effectively, no one will ever reject you again.

5. **Go to the next step.** The next step is to schedule a follow-up. It may be to calendar a meeting or schedule a face-to-face appointment, but it is critical to schedule something. You have an open window to move toward the next step in the process. Simply say, "Great! When would you like to meet?" Pin the prospect down to a specific day and time to talk. Make a follow-up appointment. You don't want to chase them down to follow up.

One of my clients recently did a great job of recapping and trial closing. His client said, "Yes, let's do it." Then my client said, "Great! I'll call you sometime next week." Big mistake. After five follow-up phone calls to schedule the next meeting, the potential client forgot the conversation and lost interest.

Recommitting Your Client

Another reason to recap and trial-close is to remind your prospect or client of their own needs. As I've noted before, people forget 70 percent of what they hear or see after one day and 90 percent after three days. There's a high likelihood that if your follow-up meeting is more than three days out, the client or prospect will barely remember the conversation. But if they are hard to reach and you leave several voicemails, it's because their motivation has dwindled as much as their memory.

With every voicemail, remind clients of their three needs. For example, "Hi, John. This is Kerry Johnson. I would love to meet on Thursday at ten o'clock to discuss the concerns we spoke about last week. These are running out of money, volatility, and taxes. You mentioned these were important to you. Please give me a call back so that we can talk more. My telephone number is xxx-xxx-xxxx."

If you use this kind of voicemail, you will reconnect and remind your prospect or client of why you are meeting. In our research over decades, we discovered that even people who have concerns will cancel a follow-up meeting 25 percent of the time. The only reason for this is a poor memory: they can't remember why they are meeting with you. It's really important to keep reminding people of their concerns and needs.

Segmenting Your Client Base

Whenever I get a new coaching client, I always ask about their own clients. I ask them to segment their clients into A, B, and

C categories. Most of my coaching clients have an idea of who their best clients are, but they've never taken the time to separate them into whom they should be spending the most time with. Most coaching clients waste a lot of time doing paperwork and administration chores over clients who will not produce much business.

Often the clients who pay you the least, demand the most. They are often the neediest. They often call text and email frequently, asking for things they could do themselves. Service equals sales. Great service often creates the greatest increase in advocacy referrals, but an increase in service to the wrong clients will only get you more low-level clients. You will still get referrals, but not to those you want to be referred to.

Let's segment your client base. Let's find out the clients you should be spending the most time talking to. Clients fit three categories:

A CLIENTS

This category consists of people who have given you the revenue or commissions that you are looking for. Often when I create a business plan with a new client, I ask what their average commission is. What they tell me is always 30–50 percent higher than reality. But if you average out the top 15 percent of your client base, you'll get a good amount of your top compensation.

Are they currently advocates? Have they referred somebody to you in the last thirty days? The answer is probably no, because you have not been asking for referrals. By definition, you can't make them A clients.

Do you enjoy them? Are they fun to talk to? Are they uplifting and enjoyable? Do you look forward to calling them every three months? Do they challenge you? Or do they sometimes stress you out?

We are looking for 15 percent. This is the percentage of people likely to fit in the A category. It's probable that not even 15 percent of your clients that fit this definition. Our goal is to turn as many of your B-level clients into A's as possible.

B CLIENTS

These are the clients you would like to make into A's. They could also give you a higher income or fee. They are capable but have not yet invested in you. They are also the kind of clients who could refer you to the kind of prospects who would build your business. They are enjoyable and fun. We look forward to talking to them on each three-month phone call. When you do get referrals from these clients, the leads are often qualified and productive. Your goal is to provide a valuable relationship and enough service to make them into A's.

C CLIENTS

These clients are frequently high-maintenance and difficult. You often think of transferring them to other colleagues or associates. They will never be able to give you the fees and commissions that will meet your goals, no matter how great your service and no matter how much time you spend with them. Here's *the* most important part: if you do get referrals from these people, you will only get more C clients. You've undoubtedly heard that birds of a feather flock together. There's a lot of truth to this: we all make within 10 and 20 percent of our best friends' incomes. Most of my best friends are small-business owners or professionals who play tennis or golf. This is because I see them when we participate in these sports. I play tennis or golf nearly every day. It's really easy to maintain a relationship when you play tennis together or during a four-hour golf round.

Only the more affluent are willing to pay $300 a month for a tennis club membership or $75 for an afternoon round of golf. Coincidentally, nearly every one of my tennis buddies providing a referral is qualified.

I also get referrals from other sources: sometimes my church friends and people I meet at parties. Some 50 to 75 percent of these people are very nice but will produce absolutely no business. When a C client or a nonsports friend introduces me, I simply ask a lot of qualifying questions.

What should you do with C-level clients? Transfer them to associates and colleagues who could use more business. It's all about what your time is worth.

How Much Is Your Time Worth?

The simple answer is to divide your overall gross income by 1600 hours worked in a year. A far more effective way to calculate your time is to divide your income by the amount of time you talk to A and B level clients. As you might have guessed, your income is only as high as the amount of time you spend talking to clients. Anything you can delegate can't be counted as time well spent.

One of my clients is a home-based small business owner. He said he can't afford to hire an assistant. At $20 an hour, it would cost too much. Doing a deeper dive, he made $200 an hour when he spoke to clients. Anything besides client communication dropped his income to $20 an hour. This is the amount of money he made doing nonclient communication work. He was trading $200 an hour for a $20 an hour job. I don't like those averages, do you? His mindset was so stuck in thrift that he actually asked me if he should pay a job candidate $22 an hour instead of $20. I had a long talk with him to change his mindset. We had to talk about the activities producing the most amount of money.

During the 1992 recession, my business was in a downturn. Two years earlier, I had bought a house that desperately needed paint. I spent almost a week scraping the ivy off the walls and prepping for paint. After five twelve-hour days, I did an acceptable but not a great job. A month later, I met a painter and told him about all my hard work. I asked how much he would have charged. He said $1,800. That's it. I spent 80 hours on the job. My time doing that was worth $22.50 an hour. What would my time have been worth spent marketing? Perhaps $200 an hour? Lesson learned.

With your C-level clients, I recommend having a conversation with them explaining that you will keep in contact, but less frequently. You want to provide great service. You can achieve that goal by having a colleague or associate call them more often. Physician assistants are a wonderful service for medical doctors. They can often do medical histories and initial diagnoses. This makes the physician-patient time even more productive, and the physician is still in contact with the patient. I've never heard anyone say the doctor needs to gather the information that the physician assistant is capable of.

This should be your service goal. You need to become the clients' high-impact doctor. Hire your own "physician assistant."

Call Your A and B Clients Frequently

The goal is to contact your A and B clients at least every three months, if not more. Since B clients are capable of giving you quality referrals and becoming A's with more frequent contact, treat them like A's. Since A's are willing and capable of giving you advocacy referrals, give them your best service and focus on building the relationship.

You will also discover that transferring your C's to somebody else will improve service to the top-level A and B clients. This is really getting into the weeds, since most customers and clients are never called after the sale. The process of contacting clients will make you more focused on building a relationship and referrals.

Always Ask for Referrals

The last step is asking for referrals. If you make a three-month phone call and schedule a follow-up, save the referral request for your follow-up meeting. But if you can't find the needs and value that the client is seeking, it's critical to discuss referrals while you are talking.

The Two Kinds of Referrals

There are two kinds of referrals:

1. **Proactive.** These are referrals you get as a result of making contact like in a three-month phone call. You have learned to ask for people they know who could benefit from the kinds of things you've done for them. There is a 38 percent chance the referred lead you receive will book an appointment with you.

2. **Advocacy.** An advocacy referral is when a client calls you directly with a name and ask you to call their friend. Or the friend calls and mentions your client. An advocacy referral has an 85 percent chance of booking business. The only way to get an advocacy referral is to keep in contact with your clients every three months and consistently ask.

The difference between proactive and advocacy referrals is not competence. It isn't your brilliance. It isn't even that you're better than all your competitors. It's frequency of contact. It's how often you keep in contact with the client using the three-month phone call.

Here are the things to say:

1. **Reestablish the relationship.** Let the client know how much you value them. As I've said, the relationship is 89 percent of the reason they did business with you in the beginning. Let them know how much the relationship means to you: "I really enjoy working with you."

2. **Let them know it's important to help their friends.** No matter what you've heard, your clients care only minimally about

building your business. They care a lot more about their own friends and family, so why not ask them to help these people? "I'm not sure you know this, but 83 percent of your friends and family will be dependent on Social Security sometime during their lives." Or: "Your friends and family will buy a home every seven years. Rarely does a realtor keep in contact. In fact, most realtors get about 10 percent below market value and take 30 percent longer to sell a home." If you are in the car business, you might say, "Your friends and family will buy a car every five years. They will lease a car every three years. Most are paying 25 percent more on the lease and 15 percent too much on a purchase."

3. **Be very direct in your request.** At first, 90 percent of my coaching clients say, "Don't keep me a secret," or, "If you know anybody, give me a call." These kinds of requests will never get good referrals. Your client will always say, "Fine," or, "I always talk about you." But they never do or will.

Instead say, "Whom do you know who could benefit from some of the things we've done so far?" If you've kept in close contact every three months, you might want to underscore the relationship by saying, "Whom do you know who could benefit from the kind of relationship we've had so far?" Either way, you will build a referral base for the future.

It's important to remember that 38 percent of your three-month phone calls will result in either a booked appointment or referrals. If you're not hitting 38 percent, you are talking too much. When you make these client or prospect phone calls, 80 percent of the time should be listening and 20 percent talking. I've never seen a client with less than a 38 percent success rate who listened too much. Instead they always make the mistake of trying to talk their clients and prospects into something.

Calling Prospects and Clients

Never cold-call. Cold calling has a 4 percent closing ratio on booking appointments. It's a poor use of time. You have too many past prospects and people in your network to need to make a cold call. In fact, my definition of a great salesperson is one who possesses the ability to make cold calls but never needs to.

The difference between a three-month client call and a prospect call is only one skill set: after the update and after you ask how they feel, remind the prospect of their three needs from the last phone call. Then move on. For example: "How does all this make you feel? "A little nervous. I should've made some changes a few years ago." Then remind them of the three needs from the last conversation: "The last time we spoke, you were very concerned about volatility, running out of money, and taxes. What have you done so far to find solutions to these concerns?" Ninety percent of the time, they've procrastinated and done nothing. Do a little hurt and rescue, then ask if they are concerned. The next steps are recap, trial close, and book a follow-up appointment.

I recommend that you call any prospect who remembers your name. Call anyone in your network and use the three-month phone call script. If you do this effectively, your sales will increase by 38 percent, and you will never make a cold call again. Nobody will ever reject you for the rest of your career, because you will never offer an appointment unless somebody provides three needs and commits to a solution.

Avoid asking for referrals on a prospect or network call. Reserve these kinds of conversations for clients. There are very advanced ways of getting referrals from nonclients, but for now make your calls every day and reestablish existing relationships.

Make Referred Lead Calls Immediately

The more quickly you act on referred leads, the more referrals you will get. Referrals are not like old wine and good cheese. It's really important to call them within twenty-four hours of getting the lead. At least leave a voicemail.

There are two reasons to call as quickly you can. First, you need the motivation to pick up the telephone. If you wait a couple days, the contact will never be made. The second reason is that your referral source is likely to send a note or text to the referred lead. If you wait too long, the referred lead will forget about you. You will also disappoint the referral source. They take pride in giving you referrals. They want you to succeed.

When you contact a referred lead, send a note immediately to the referral source. They may reach out to their friend, or even call and ask if they've spoken with you.

Years ago, I got a referral to a New York Life Insurance Company manager in San Francisco. I left a voicemail and an email immediately. (My strategy is to call and send emails three times before I give up.) Each time I made a call to the lead, I also sent a note to the referral source to let him know of my progress. After the second phone call, my referral source called the manager and asked why he had not spoken to me. The insurance company manager immediately sent an email asking if I could speak with him the next day.

Get your referral source engaged. They want to help you make contact. If you ignore them or leave them out, you will discourage referrals in the future.

"I Want to Call Them First"

Sometimes a client or referral source will say they talk about you all the time. Or they would rather call the lead first. This is a good sign. We want them to call. An introduction makes your call more effective. In fact, I ask nearly every referral source if they will send an email or note to the referred lead before I talk to them.

The problem is that sometimes this request becomes an excuse. They say they want to call somebody as a deflection. Sometimes they worry you will embarrass them. You and I both know that anybody you call will be receptive. You will always be appropriate and usually elegant. Your response to "Let me call them first" simply needs to be, "Great. Thank you so much. Whom are you thinking of?"

Another way of deflecting this response is saying, "Thank you so much for contacting them first. Would you mind if I make contact after you call them?"

Any one of these responses will work. If you get the name of a potential referral, you can remind your client during the next three-month phone call. You and I both know that the client is unlikely to call the referred lead as promised. But when you talk to the client during the next call, it'll remind them of their commitment. They will give you the name on the spot.

Another block you may get when asking for referrals is, "I will pass your name around to the right people." This is also a deflection. They will never mention you to anybody. My response is always, "Great, thank you so much! Who are you thinking of?" Most of the time they will say, "I will have to check for the right person." This is simply confirmation that they didn't have a name to begin with. It's good to push a little harder. If they need to check for the right person, send a follow-up note immediately after the telephone conversation to remind them of the commitment.

Quid pro Quo

Has anybody ever offered a referral, but only if you give them a discount first? I've been a professional speaker presenting around the world for more than forty years. I often receive offers for referrals but only if I speak for free or for a discount. This has never worked out well. Referrals you have to buy are never as good as the ones you earn. Purchased referrals and quid pro quo referrals almost always turn out badly.

Many years ago, Steve Levy from the New England Life Insurance Company asked me to speak on a complimentary basis to his Northern California agency. (The New England has since been purchased by another company.) Steve said he was on the committee to pick the company's national convention speaker as well as their management speaker. If I did his presentation for free, he would book me for the keynote slot at both of these meetings. I agreed and did a two-hour presentation to his agency, followed by a standing ovation. After the meeting, I asked Steve for his part of the agreement. He admitted that he was only one person on the committee but would talk to the program chair. He would get back to me. Predictably, he never did.

The most egregious abuse I experienced also took place many years ago. It involved a network marketing group selling legal services called Pre-Paid Legal. One of the national directors asked me to present to a regional group in Portland, Oregon. He said that the event was very influential in the company and would result in my booking at least ten speeches to other regions around the country.

I again did a great job and got a standing ovation. Immediately after the presentation, the executive took me out for a drink and tried to recruit me into their network as a salesperson. He said if I was in their network, it would be a lot easier for me to get speeches. They never intended to give me names of other regions; they only wanted to recruit me to their network. The worst part was, I had paid for my own airfare and hotel to speak. (The more mistakes I make, the more I learn, and the wiser I get.)

How do you avoid the quid pro quo pitch? The answer is a simple negotiation technique: always get the referral before the service is rendered. Personally, I would never do a presentation in exchange for a referral. But if I did, I would want the referral ahead of time.

The Five Steps to Gaining Referrals

So far, we've spoken about how to get referrals during your three-month phone calls. Let's do a deeper dive now on the five steps in generating a constant stream of referrals. Unlike the sentences used with the three-month phone call each of these five steps not only encompasses a mindset of consistently thinking about referrals but also gives you a skill set to build referral conversations.

1. **Always be asking and thinking about referrals.**

Make referrals part of every conversation. The only way to develop the huge benefits of advocacy is to create a mindset toward referrals. In 1983, I was hired by Anchor National Financial to speak at five regional meetings. After the fifth program, Charlie Shafer, the president, asked if I accepted referrals. I said, "Of course, Charlie. Why do you mention this?" He said, "Because you've never asked. I didn't think you wanted them." I wanted to shoot myself in the head. Charlie gave me five referrals to other companies on his network. I booked all five groups for presentations. My lack of a referral mindset nearly cost me $30,000. I was focused on the existing presentation and not enough on new business. I neglected thinking about referrals for the future.

You need to be thinking about referrals in every interaction. Whether it's a client or new prospect, think, "Is this the kind of person that I would like referrals from? Is this someone who could introduce me to people like them?"

2. **The personal touch.**

This is probably one of the most important things to ask when you get a referral. Most of the time you will contact a referred lead referencing the referral source. If you are good, you're likely to say, "My name is Kerry Johnson. We have a mutual friend named John Smith. I would love to sit down and talk to you about some of the things that I do."

This script will get you a whopping 10 percent closing ratio. The reason it's so low is a lack of rapport and trust on the telephone. In fact, it's likely to backfire. If your client calls the lead and asked how the call went, the friend will likely say, "Why did you give my name to him?" This is one of the reasons people don't like to give referrals. If it doesn't go well, the client will be embarrassed.

A much more effective strategy is to ask something about the referred lead in advance. When you get a referral, ask about something unique. Do they play tennis? Do they play golf? How many kids do they have? Is there something special about them?

One of my clients asked a referral source about something special regarding the referral lead. He said his friend went deer hunting and ended up face-to-face with a buffalo. Not knowing what to do, he fired his gun in the air, and the buffalo ran away. On the referred lead phone call, my client mentioned the buffalo as an icebreaker. The referred lead was impressed that my client knew so much about him and booked an appointment.

Many years ago, a mortgage broker called referred by my lawyer, Alan. He said that my name came up, and he wanted to know if I'd thought of refinancing my house. But before asking, he mentioned hearing that I was a past pro tennis player. He asked if I ever played John McEnroe. I said, "No, McEnroe was three years after me." He asked if I'd played anybody famous. I told him that I lost to the best. We both laughed.

I looked at my watch and noticed that we had spent ten minutes talking about tennis. I didn't have any plans to refinance my house, but I was thinking about building a second story and asked if the rep did bridge loans. We started the application. There was no way I would have started the process had he not built rapport. I was not in the market to refinance, and I would not have thought about a home equity line of credit unless the sales rep developed enough rapport first.

Surprisingly, I ended up using another mortgage company, because the rep's boss refused to return my phone calls. I wrote monthly for a major mortgage magazine, and she was one of the top mortgage professionals in America. Although the rep was responsive, she was not. If she refused to talk as the head of the company, I would only be a transaction, not a relationship. This let me know that their culture wasn't one that valued clients. If their rates had been way below those of the competition, perhaps I would have done the deal. But if you have competition, you'd better have pretty good sales skills.

3. Listen for referrals.

I get about five referrals every day, although I haven't directly asked for any in years. That's because I always listen for opportunities. I always listen for people name-dropping their friends, family, and colleagues. My definition of a brilliant sales producer is somebody who has the ability to ask for referrals but never has to. Your clients will always name-drop. Your friends will always mention people they know. All you have to do is ask for a name. Then, at the end of the conversation, ask if you can contact them. This is the easiest way to gain referrals.

I was on the phone recently with the editor of the magazine of the Million Dollar Round Table. She had read one of my articles in another publication and asked if she could reprint it. I offered to write monthly articles, which would save her a lot of time contacting other writers. She was really grateful.

The Million Dollar Round Table is the insurance industry's premier level sales organization, with members around the world. She asked if I knew about their three major events during the year. Of course I did; I'd spoken at two of them already. I said, "Who runs those events?" We talked for a few more minutes about the attendees and locations. Then she looked up the event scheduled for November. At the end of the conversation I asked for the meeting planner's name and some contact information. I got the name, email, and a phone number. I just listened. I didn't have to ask.

One of my clients recently did a three-month phone call with one of his clients. At first, he did a catch-up and then an economic update. The client said he had a friend with an interesting view of the economy. My client asked more about the friend. They played golf together frequently. The friend ran a small business. My client even got a name, John. At the end of the call, my client said he would love to contact John and got an email and telephone number. The client freely gave it to him.

Again, the best way to get referrals is to simply listen. You don't always have to have a great referral script. Clients will always name-drop. They will always talk about the friends and colleagues. All you have to do is pay attention and ask questions.

Perhaps the biggest mistake my clients make is talking too much. People don't buy because they're sold; they buy because they sell themselves. People buy not because they're made to understand; they buy because they feel understood.

The more you listen, the more referrals you get. When you hear a client talk about needs, ask more questions. When you hear a client talk about friends, ask for names. When you hear a prospect talk about goals, ask about their plans.

The listener always controls the conversation. The more you listen, the faster you will build sales. I don't connect with people in social media unless I can talk to them on the phone or face-to-face. My goal is simply to find out more about them. I get referrals on every phone call because I listen. (We will discuss social media strategy in chapter 8.) But 80 percent of any client contact time should be listening; 20 percent should be presenting.

4. The comfort response.

Many years ago, one of my clients, Rich Rubino, said the referral strategies I taught him didn't work. He mentioned that a few of his clients didn't feel comfortable giving him names. One even explained that a network marketer embarrassed one of her friends by being too pushy. She didn't want to be put in that position ever again. So we developed a very innovative way to discover who was likely to refer and who never would.

The comfort response question is, "What would I have to do to make you feel comfortable enough to introduce me to your friends, colleagues, and family?" This is a very assertive way of asking for referrals, but if you can make the request in an elegant way, you will earn the right to get them. You will also find out those who will never give you names, no matter how much you ask. There are two general responses to this kind of request:

1. "If you will help me save money and keep in contact every few months, I will give you names of all the people I know."
2. "I'd rather not. I've had some bad experiences in the past."

Either way, the method works. If you find out the client's goals and names after the sale, you win. If the client prefers not to give referrals, they become C-level clients. You will call them once a year, but you won't ask for referrals in the future.

"What would I have to do . . . ?" may come off as too pushy. Here is a more elegant way to ask: "Most of my business is word-of-mouth. I really love my clients. We are like family. What would I have to do over the next few weeks to make you feel comfortable enough to introduce me to some of your friends and family?"

With this approach, rarely will anybody feel pushed, pressed, or sold to. They will recognize there is a pathway to becoming your client that is exclusive and beneficial. In addition, the more referrals you get, the more your clients refer. Those clients who come to you from a referral tend in turn to refer more people to you, because that is how connected with you in the first place. Referrals beget more referrals.

5. Ask for introductions rather than referrals.

Sometimes a simple word is backed by a lot of emotion. The names Stacey, Caroline, Catherine, Benji, Cora, and Merita are meaningless to you. But they are the precious names of my wife, kids, and grandkids and are very special to me.

Every salesperson uses the word *referral*. If there is ever a bad experience, it is based on the representation of referrals, not of introductions. My friends introduce me to other friends. They say, "I'd like you to meet . . ." They don't say, "I want to refer you to my friend John."

Realtors, insurance agents, and chiropractors ask for referrals, not introductions. My lawyer is likely to introduce me to another lawyer. My physician is likely to introduce me to a specialist. My CPA is likely to introduce me to an estate planning attorney. So let's start replacing the word *referral* with *introduction*.

Years ago, I came home to my wife asking to pay the carpet cleaner. He did a good job and pointed at some dark stains he was able to clean. He then asked to be referred to my neighbors for carpet cleaning services. It hit me immediately that if a carpet cleaner asks for a referral, the rest of us ought to ramp up our game. We'd better start using the word *introduction* instead.

Perhaps the client has had a bad experience in the past with referrals. More likely they had a good experience with introductions. Emotions could be all in a word.

Many years ago, I spoke at the Louisiana conference of the American Institute of Certified Public Accountants (AICPA). Accountants have terrible sales skills. Although most of them want to build a practice, they don't want to hear about sales. I had to change my topic from "Sales Magic" to "How to Read Your Client's Mind." Physicians are exactly the same. And I once spoke to a bar association and got similar pushback.

With these professionals, talk about building a practice, but don't use the word *sales*. Use the word *relationships* instead of *sales*. At the AICPA conference, I still spoke about prospecting, probing, presenting, and closing. But instead of sales jargon, I substituted the words *origination*, *fact finding*, *solutions*, and *implementation*. Why these professionals have such an aversion to sales is beyond me. After all, before people make money, something has to be sold.

This is also the case with introductions. For example, "Whom can you introduce me to?" Or, "I would love to be introduced to John. Do you have any contact information for him?" Or even, "I would love to meet Jennifer. Would you mind introducing me to her?"

Introduction Notes

Speaking of introductions, it's a wonderful idea to ask the referral source to send a note of introduction. This is a little controversial, since your client may talk about something the referred lead cares little about. For example, they may talk about how good you are at protecting their retirement account when the referred lead may not have a need for retirement. Or they may talk about what a great job you did on their carpeting when the referral is really looking for hardwood flooring. But on balance, an introductory call from your client is much better than your contacting them out of the blue.

No matter what system you use, don't accept the client's offer to forward something. They won't. You may hear, "Give me your card, and I will send it to them." They won't. Always get a name. We actually want them to forward information about you. We just want a referral name to follow up with.

4

What to Say to Referred Leads

Referrals are like gold, but most producers squander the opportunity. When they finally reach the referred lead, they say, "We should meet sometime." Or they leave an innocuous voicemail that merely mentions the referral source and pitches an appointment: "You and I both know John Smith. Please call me back. I'd like to book an appointment to see you." The referred lead doesn't know who you are and will rarely meet with you just because you both know the same person.

Five Steps in Contacting Referred Leads

Here are five steps that will help book appointments with referred leads. If you use these steps, 38 percent of the referred leads will book an appointment with you, but only if you learn and use them.

1. Introduction.
2. Personal touch.

3. The elevator speech.

4. The four-step bridge.

5. Book and calendar an appointment.

INTRODUCTION

Introduce yourself, name your company and referral source, and engage the prospect within seven seconds. As soon as the other person answers he telephone, mention who you are and the name of your company. For example, "My name is Kerry Johnson. I'm a financial advisor with Merrill Lynch. You and I have a mutual friend, John Smith. You know John Smith, don't you?"

As soon as you mention your mutual friend, the lead will probably become enthusiastic or at least acknowledge the person with a comment. For example, "I haven't seen John in months. How is he doing?"

Get the prospect to engage within the first few sentences. I get these phone calls a couple of times a week. Most of the salespeople introduce themselves, mention our mutual friend, but then ruin the call by going on for five minutes about what they do. As they talk, I usually become distracted by my emails and texts and generally ignore them. It's critical to get them to interact with you in the first seven seconds.

PERSONAL TOUCH

The next critical part of the call is the personal touch. I've already mentioned how important it is to learn something unique about the referred lead. Do they play golf? Do they play tennis? Did they just get back from a vacation? Do they have a valedictorian in the family? Do they just have a new grandkid? This will buy you at least ten minutes on the telephone to develop rapport.

Whenever I get a referral, I ask something unique about the person. I recently received a wonderful referral to a meeting planner. The first thing I asked was how well my referral source knew them; could they tell me something unique? The first response was their job title. I then stressed, "Can you tell me something special? Something that is fun about them?" My referral source said the lead just got a new Peloton and was addicted to it. Now that's pretty unique. When I made a phone call, I said, "Jill just said you get a new Peloton workout machine. Congratulations. How often do you use it?"

She replied by asking if I knew much about Pelotons. We spent ten minutes talking about how she uses it every morning before work. She even mentioned how she is connected to other people during her rides. I can honestly say that not one person has ever blown me off the telephone when I use the personal touch discussion.

You can also use the personal touch in a voicemail or even a follow-up email. I will frequently mention something special in an email to a referred lead. Sometimes when the referred lead is unresponsive to a voicemail, I will mention something special. For example, "By the way John, I just heard you got a new Corvette. Congratulations." It is unlikely you will be ignored you if you know that much about the person you are calling.

THE ELEVATOR SPEECH

The next mistake producers make is to try to book an appointment too quickly. They often think the referred lead needs their services so badly that they will book an appointment without knowing anything about them. That is a mistake. Nobody is just sitting around the telephone waiting to do business simply because you called. They are busy and need a reason to meet with you. It's also likely that affluent prospects already work with somebody who does what you do. You have to give them a reason to meet that fills a need. The way to do this is with an elevator speech.

The elevator speech frames the discussion, presents the outline of the conversation, and establishes credibility. You need to build an elevator speech that sells what you do.

An elevator speech has the following parts:

Label yourself, so they don't have to.

After the personal touch, ask if the referral source mentioned anything about you. For example, "Did John say anything about me? Do you mind if I give you some background?" If you are in a business-to-business relationship, you can use the words "elevator speech." For example, "Do you mind if I give you a quick elevator speech?"

Businesspeople all know what an elevator speech is, but nobody knows how to do it effectively. They will be very impressed when you deliver one. If you're a financial advisor, say so. If you are a solar energy consultant, mention it. If you are a mortgage rep, let them know. Don't make them guess. You do not want somebody to say, "So you are kind of like a —, right?"

Sometimes I hear creative labels like a "retirement salvation specialist," or I hear mortgage brokers describe themselves as "cash flow specialists." This only confuses the prospect. They're trying to put you into a format to make sense of what you do. It's not bad to say you are a retirement salvation specialist, as long as you've let them know ahead of time that you are a financial advisor. Many decades ago, I called myself a sales psychologist. I would constantly get a quizzical look with the response, "So you are kind of like a consultant, right?" In my attempt to be unique, I only confused the prospect.

Let them know three things you do better than anybody on earth. An elevator speech is often confusing. It is usually long-winded and hard to follow. For example, "I work with realtors and homeowners to get a good mortgage no matter the situation they're in, using the right credit score and helping them pick the right loan depending on how long they might be in the property."

When you use a long-winded description, your prospect actually hears nothing. Break your description into three succinct points. The simpler you can make it, the longer they will remember it. For example, "I do three things for my clients. First, I make sure they never run out of money during retirement. Next, I make sure volatility never has an impact. Thirdly, my clients always minimize their tax payment."

A realtor might say, "I do three things: First, I make sure clients get the highest price. My clients also sell their homes quicker than any other competitor. And third, I talk to them frequently to make sure they are always in the loop."

If you're a car salesperson, you might say, "I do three things for my clients: I get the lowest price for exactly the car they want. Second, we provide better warranties than any other competitor.

And third, we keep in contact with our clients frequently to make sure the vehicle performs as expected."

The whole purpose of the elevator speech is to differentiate yourself from all your competitors. I had a client recently who thought the elevator speech took too long. He said clients already know what he did. That may be true, but I want to frame the conversation so that the prospect knows the unique things I do better than anybody else. I also want to structure the conversation by focusing on what I do best.

I have three elevator speeches: one as a speaker, one as a business coach, and one as an author. For example, "I do three things other speakers don't. First, I give the audiences ideas they can use immediately to improve their business. Number two, I make sure they are entertained to increase their memory of the presentation points. Lastly, I make sure that the audience participates every five to ten minutes."

Every meeting planner has had a bad speaker experience. They know what great speakers do and what makes them effective. When I can frame the conversation in terms of what they want in a great speaker, the conversation becomes much more successful.

Tell a story.

The only thing people remember in an elevator speech is the story. Facts tell; stories sell. If you can wrap up your three benefits into a story, the prospect will emotionally connect with you. They will not only hear what differentiates you, but apply it. Make sure the story takes less than ninety seconds. Long stories only become boring, not informative. I've never heard a story in all my decades that I could not abbreviate. The only important things to discuss in a story are three benefits, the person's name, and occupation. Everything else you can fill in. For example, "I do three things for my clients. First, I make sure they never run out of money during retirement. Secondly, I make sure that volatility never has an impact. Finally, I make sure my clients minimize taxes in their golden years.

"One of my clients is Donna. She was a schoolteacher for thirty-five years. Divorced recently, she was nervous about market volatility. I put her into a very safe investment with a guaranteed income. Even though the market tanked by 35 percent, she did not lose a penny. She came by my office recently with my favorite chai tea latte and a Bundt cake that she made herself. She sat down, lowered her eyeglasses and said, 'If it wasn't for you, I don't think I would have survived the last few months. Thank God I found you.' When I can help clients like this, I know it's all worthwhile."

This is an example of illustrating what you do with a story that will never be forgotten. Stories are everything. I have clients who remember my stories years after I tell them. But if I asked them for steps in the process, they are often lost. Stories are everything.

The takeaway.

After you've labeled yourself and engaged, used the personal touch, and done the elevator speech, use the takeaway. Its purpose is to let listeners know what you do without pitching. It ensures that the prospect will never feel sold to.

An example of the takeaway is, "I'm not sure this will benefit you, but I'd like to find out more about you first." Another way of saying this is, "I don't know if this is something you need, but I'd like to learn more about you first."

The takeaway will make the prospect less defensive and will better engage them in the conversation. Some people say they want to be more candid to earn the right to work with me. When people don't feel sold to, they are more honest and forthcoming. When they feel pitched, they grow defensive. Make it a friendly conversation, not a sales process. Take all the sales jargon you have learned and toss it in the trash. Make referrals a conversation you might have with a friend.

Here's how an elevator speech sounds put together: "Mr. Smith? My name is Kerry Johnson. I'm a financial advisor with Johnson Financial. We have a mutual friend named Bud Brandt. You know Bud, don't you? He tells me you're a long-range cyclist. That must be fun. Where have you gone? Did Bud say anything about me?"

"Can I give you a quick elevator speech? I do three things for my clients. First, I make sure they never run out of money during retirement. Second, no matter how bad the market volatility, my clients never lose a penny. And third, I keep in contact with my clients frequently to provide market updates and check to maintain they are on track to meet their retirement goals.

"One of my clients, John, is a retired midlevel manager with IBM. In March 2020, during the Covid-19 financial crisis, the stock market lost 36 percent, but my client didn't lose a penny. In fact, he sent me a gift card for Fleming's steakhouse as a way of saying thanks. Fleming's didn't open up for months later, so I couldn't use it for a while, but that was his way of saying thanks. All his friends were spending sleepless nights worrying. I'm not sure that will help you at all, but I like to find out more about you first."

THE FOUR-STEP BRIDGE

Another huge mistake most producers make is to pitch an appointment much too soon. Many sales pros listen just long enough to sell something. They then immediately try to book an appointment without establishing any need. They think the referral is sitting by the phone dying to meet them. That is absolutely not true. Prospects will never be so impressed by what you say that they can't wait to book an appointment. They're extremely busy and are looking for a way to blow you off the phone. You have to give them a reason to meet that is overwhelming.

The answer is the four-step bridge. It is so effective that you will never be rejected again. You can think of it as a way to "listen people into appointments." The process involves closing without closing, pitching without pitching. It is the psychotherapeutic model of selling.

Good psychologists don't tell you what to do. They have talked to people like you a thousand times. They know the answers to your issues after the first sentence. Even though they know the solution, they keep their mouths shut. They want you to discover the solution, so they prompt you by asking the right questions. These pros help you discover the right path on your own. The good ones then hold you accountable to implement what you've learned. This is what the four-step bridge is all about. Here are the steps:

Introductory statement.

First engage the referred lead. The transition could be the elevator speech takeaway. You could say, "I'm not sure this will benefit you, but I'd like to find out more about you first." Another introductory sentence could be, "Tell me about your retirement plan. Do you have one? Are your market returns on track to hit your retirement goals?"

Whenever I don't know what to say, I ask questions. Whenever I get confused, I ask questions. Whenever I need more time, I ask questions. If I get a phone call from someone who wants to buy a book, I ask how they know me. If someone wants to know about my presentation topics, I ask about their meeting goals first. I will never present a solution until I find needs.

Get three needs.

As I've mentioned already, research has shown that one need produces a 36 percent closing ratio. Two needs results in a 56 percent chance of a sale. Three needs equals a 92 percent chance of getting their business. You should always be looking for three needs.

Recap their needs.

Restate their three needs as a psychotherapist would. Again, 86 percent of buyers don't only want to understand; they want to be understood. If you can listen to their goals and develop rapport, they are much more likely to book an appointment with you.

The trial close.

Here's an example of a trial close. "If we could take a look at avoiding running out of money, decreasing volatility, and lowering taxes, would that be helpful?"

BOOK AND CALENDAR AN APPOINTMENT

Calendar the lead for a future appointment. Often the lead will say, "Call me back next week and we can talk," or, "This sounds like a great idea. I'm busy for the next few weeks; let's talk when I have more time."

Don't fall for this. It's a trap and will waste your time. If you accept this distraction, you will dial the telephone five times before you reconnect. By the time you get them back on the phone, they will have forgotten nearly everything, and you will have to start over. Here is a much better way to handle the future appointment. "That's a great idea. When would you like to follow up? In a couple of weeks? How about the twenty-sixth at 10 a.m.? Does that work for you? I'll send you a calendar invite, and we can talk then." When you send the follow-up note, remind them of the three needs to discuss on the next appointment. The only people I don't calendar are those I don't care about following up with.

Don't let people put you off. Don't let them waste your time. If you call a referred lead in a few weeks without an appointment, it's like taking $400 out of your pocket and throwing it in the trash. Your time is too valuable to waste. Even if a referred lead doesn't want to book an appointment and says they don't have a calendar in front of them, suggest a follow-up time anyway. Let them know that if they cannot make it, they can just give you a call. There is absolutely no benefit to chasing prospects.

In most cases, prospective referred leads won't book an appointment unless there is a match. But since you never want to waste your time, it's important to qualify prospects. Some qualification questions for a financial advisor could be:

Are you currently working with a broker? If they have spoken to their broker in the last three months, they are unlikely to work with you. A current relationship is stickier than glue. Even a bad broker relationship is hard to break as long as there is frequent contact.

If they are willing to meet but have talked to their existing broker in the last three months, try to push back. This is simply asking why they would want to meet with you if they already have an advisor.

Here's a way of asking that gets results: "I'm curious about your advisor. Is it something about them that you don't like? Is there something about that relationship you would like to improve?"

One of my friends, insurance sales star Van Mueller, has a great line for booking referred lead appointments with those who have a current relationship with a competitor. Van's response is, "Do you have enough faith in your existing broker to get a second opinion?" He swears by this line and says it gains many appointments. All Van wants to do is get past the reflex response. He knows his services are better than those of any of his competitors. He only wants to get in front of a prospect to gain an at bat.

What is your career, and how long have you been there? If you have not yet already asked, find out the referred lead's career before you meet. If I were to give you five jobs with the length of time in each one, you should be able to tell me how much money this person makes and how much they have in retirement assets. For example, a midlevel manager with IBM probably makes $175,000 and has $500,000 in assets. A thirty-five-year-old schoolteacher probably makes $85,000 with a guaranteed retirement income of $5,000 a month. A florist with three shops and more than ten years' experience as an owner probably makes $150,000 a year and is hoping to sell the business for $500,000 to retire on. Here's a great way to ask: "You sound very educated. What you do for living?" Asking this will get all the information you need.

Did you lose any money in the last recession? Financial advisors usually want to know where money is right now. Some folks may have exited the market during the last downturn. In any case, this question will usually elicit a discussion to give you more information. If you can ask if they lost any money in the last recession, it will show whether they have been in the stock market. If they say no, they may have invested in real estate, bonds, or precious metals. Regardless, they will tell you where their assets are.

Don't book appointments with people who can't buy. It's very tempting to book an appointment with a referred lead, no matter what the cost. It is difficult enough to get a referral; then it's hard to get the person on the telephone. When you eventually make contact, you feel lucky. You have a laser lock on booking an appointment. But you need to be protective of your time: you should only meet with people as long as there is a benefit to you both. If they're not qualified, you shouldn't book an appointment.

If there's no benefit, maybe you can do some pro bono work. But do not waste your time. It is much too valuable.

Leaving Voicemails

It's highly likely that you will be unable to reach the referred lead on the first attempt. Some producers think they should keep dialing until they reach someone. That's a mistake. Leaving too many messages is problematic. Every voicemail advertises that you've called.

It's also a mistake to leave a long voicemail. The more information you give, the more they can filter to decide whether or not to call you back. An example of a bad voicemail is, "My name is Kerry Johnson, from Johnson Financial. We have a mutual friend, John Smith. John mentioned that you have a retirement account and may need some help. I like to talk to you more about what you are invested in and whether I can help increase returns. Please call me back at xxx-xxx-xxxx."

This voicemail may seem complete. It may also seem descriptive. But an abbreviated voicemail will get many more return calls than a long, drawn-out one. Here's an example of an appropriate voicemail that will get twice as many return calls: "Hi, Mr. Smith. My name is Kerry Johnson, from Johnson Financial. Please call me back regarding Don Thompson. My phone number is xxx-xxx-xxxx. I look forward to hearing from you."

The more information you leave in the voicemail, the more likely the referred lead is to filter your call. If they don't think they need your services, you will not get a call back. But if you leave a message regarding a mutual friend, they will not know the context of the call, and you are more likely to get a return. You goal is to talk. Then you can find needs and learn whether you can help.

It's also important to follow your voicemail with an email. It's easy to ignore a voicemail, but it's not as easy to ignore an email. In fact, in their response they may ask what the call is about. You can simply deflect the question by asking in turn to talk for ten minutes. Above all, you need to avoid the referred lead's attempt to screen you. Instead spend ten minutes getting to know them.

5

The Wedge

WHAT TO DO WHEN THEY ALREADY HAVE A VENDOR

The most difficult objection to overcome in a referred lead call is, "I already have a vendor." This strikes fear in the heart of any sales pro. Very few know what to say. Sometimes you're likely to tell them how good you are or how much better you are than their current vendor. At other times, you may simply ignore the response and try to book an appointment. Neither will get you anywhere.

Often the lead's mention of a current provider is a reflex response. They may mention working with somebody else only to get you off the telephone. They may also tell you they have an advisor even when that person hasn't spoken to them in years or did a bad job. Either way, it's important for you to get them to talk about the current relationship and what they would like to see improved. This process is called the *wedge*. The concept is based on three truths:

1. Most clients don't want to be sold, but they are very willing to buy.
2. People feel that the best ideas are the ones they think of themselves.
3. There are three people present in every sale: you, the prospect, and their incumbent vendor.

There Are Three of You in the Sale

One reason for a low closing ratio is thinking you are selling to only one prospect. In fact, it is always a triangle. It is always you, the prospect, and the current vendor. Even though you have a better idea, a way to save money, or even a way to solve a problem, the prospect must be willing to change. They have to be first willing to sever the relationship with their current provider. Most people have a great dependency on the status quo. There is a great likelihood they will avoid change. The status quo is always easier than the effort of making a decision.

During the 2008 recession, my client Kathy in Bend, Oregon, met with a seventy-five-year-old divorced grandmother. The prospect had lost nearly 45 percent of her portfolio when the market crashed. In tears, the potential client did not want to become a greeter at Walmart and was terrified about her future retirement. She had not spoken to her broker in ten years and needed Kathy's help. Kathy looked over the portfolio and discovered it was in risky assets, creating too much volatility, especially for a woman in her seventies. The grandmother was deeply appreciative and told Kathy she would be back the next morning with a check moving her retirement assets.

The woman did come back the next morning, without the check. She called the broker, who said to keep the money where it was. The prospect wanted to give Kathy the courtesy of telling her face-to-face. This is the power of an incumbent relationship matched with the sometimes self-sabotaging behavior of the status quo.

Getting through the Stall

Sometimes the referred lead will put you off by asking to talk some other time. That future will never come. People forget 70 percent of what they hear within one day, and 90 percent within three days. In a month from now, the referred lead will forget not only your name but even the conversation. They will stall you. They will say something like, "Give me a call in a few months; I will see how my provider does," or, "I have a provider right now. Give me your phone number, and I will call you back if something happens." You will never get that phone call.

Stalling often means that the prospect will tell you what you want to hear and then reconnect with their own provider. The provider will do everything they can to conserve business. The most powerful weapon in their arsenal is to create doubt. This will cause your potential client to avoid change and do nothing.

One financial advisor presented a retirement plan to a prospect, who was very excited and said, "I can't wait to get this started; I wish I had done this ten years ago."

But then the prospect checked in with the old advisor. At first, he said it was a wonderful idea, but then started to create doubt.

The incumbent advisor said to watch out for the hidden fees, adding that the risk is much greater than he would have recommended and that there was a great likelihood that the client is wasting money.

The client became nervous and said to the new advisor, "What about the hidden fees? Do you really think I could lose money with this?" All the incumbent advisor had to do was create doubt. The prospect was scared. Because of status quo bias, the client chose to do nothing.

The Answer

Here is the answer to this problem:

1. The prospect needs to fire the incumbent vendor in order to make the sale.
2. You first have to get the prospect to tell you what they dislike about their old vendor.
3. You have to listen to the prospect talk about their vendor relationship before you can sell a new one.

The Relationship with the Incumbent Provider

Before the prospect makes a change, they often will get one last opinion from the old provider, or they will feel compelled to tell the incumbent about moving their money. This will allow the incumbent to match your offer and sometimes improve it. The standing relationship is often stronger than a new one with you. The old provider is likely to win. All they need to do is present a product or service like yours: because of the existing relationship, they win. Your response often is to push harder with logic, but since the existing relationship is based on emotion, you lose.

If, say, you are a financial advisor, you are likely to say things like, "We can save 3 percent on commissions by doing this. You will never take a loss again with this approach. Over the last ten years, we would have increased your returns by 35 percent." These are all great arguments, but the incumbent advisor can match those benefits, and keep the relationship. After all, "The devil I know is better than the one I don't know."

The same thing can happen in a realtor, mortgage broker, CPA, or even HVAC relationship. For example, the referred lead may say, "I already have a contract with an HVAC company." When you mention a discount, they will simply call their incumbent provider and ask to match the price, so you lose. People don't change providers because of lower prices. They change because the new provider offers a better relationship.

Never Attack the Incumbent

Never attack the incumbent advisor or their current service: the prospect may feel compelled to defend them. This makes a lot of sense. "If you point out mistakes, I will justify and rationalize. I may even resent you." This will also cause the prospect to block you in the future.

Coincidentally, criticizing the competition is one of the first things you are likely to do. Recently a prospect told me about doing a radio show as a way to create new business. I told him that radio was expensive, time-consuming, and unproductive. I wanted to point out his mistake. I gave him three other ideas for creating leads that were much more effective than radio. Instead, he defended the strategy, and the conversation ended.

Here are some specific techniques you can use to implement the wedge. Remember, you cannot denigrate their current provider and expect a sale. You will always lose. Instead, get the prospect to tell you what their goals are, and ask if they are 100 percent sure that the current provider can get those results.

1. **Start with the instant replay technique.** *Instant replay* is a sports term referring to the fact the judges will look at a video replay to spot a mistake. We can also use this concept to find out how people made purchase decisions in the past, because how they behaved in the past indicates how they will behave in the future. In other words, if I can find out how you made past buying decisions, I can see how you are likely to decide in the future.

Recently a meeting planner told me she was looking for a speaker to address their five hundred salespeople. She asked what my topics were. I gave her an elevator speech, but immediately afterward I asked her who the last speaker was. I recognized the name. I was familiar with his content. He's a friend. I then asked how she decided to pick him.

"He was enthusiastic and spoke on ideas that would help our troops increase their referrals."

"What else?"

"He offered to do a webinar thirty days later to help solidify the concepts and make lasting changes."

I asked about other goals and for more background about the group. When she asked what I would do, I simply rephrased the points she mentioned in picking her last speaker.

She said, "That's exactly what we want. Are you available on July 17?"

If you can find out how people bought before, they will likely repeat that same behavior in the future.

2. **The "let's assume" technique.** This is probably the most powerful question you can ask a referred lead. If you ask it the right way, the prospect will tell you exactly what they want to buy. All you have to do then is sell it to them.

If you are a retirement specialist, you might ask, "Let's assume it's twenty years in the future. What happened that let you know all your goals were met and you had a great advisor relationship?"

Many prospects can't visualize that far ahead. They may ask you to repeat the question. But if you get them to think ahead twenty years and what goals they achieved, you will have all the information you need to produce a wedge. They may say something like, "Enough money to pay my bills." Or they could say, "I want to travel to see my grandkids every three months."

Your next response is critical. If you say this the right way, you will create a wedge. Here it is: "Are you 100 percent sure your current advisor will hit all your goals twenty years from now? Beyond a shadow of a doubt, are you totally confident they will get you there?"

The next part is critical. If they have any doubts or say something like "I'm not sure," ask what they are not sure about. It will tell you their worries and concerns. Using the five-step bridge, you will then recap, trial-close, and book an appointment.

3. **Talk about perfection.** Often prospects don't know what they want. They have a provider but have never thought about the future. It's up to you, then, to suggest possible outcomes and ask them to pick. For example, "A lot of my clients say they want to avoid running out of money, decrease volatility, and lower their taxes. Do any of these seem like goals for you?" Most prospects will pick out one as an objective or suggest their own.

When you hear their goals, ask the question again: are they 100 percent sure, beyond a shadow of a doubt, that they will get there with their current provider?

Recently a meeting planner told me she was going to use the last year's speaker for this year's convention. I told her how lucky she was to have such a great speaker presenting in back-to-back years. I then said, "Let's assume the meeting went perfectly. It's a year down the road. What happened to let you know the attendees made changes that hit your goals?"

"Their sales went up by 25 percent, they learned better closing techniques, and were more motivated than last year."

"Are you 100 percent sure, beyond a shadow of a doubt, that the speaker from last year will achieve these goals?"

"I hope so," she said.

"You don't sound terribly convinced," I replied. "Tell me your concerns."

She candidly acknowledged that because the speaker was good last year did not mean she would receive the same results by using him for the next convention. I was able to find out what her goals were and present solutions that were consistent with what she wanted to achieve.

Suggesting Perfection

Here is another way of creating a wedge by suggesting perfection. You are semisarcastically asking if the prospect has a perfect provider by sarcastically suggesting what a perfect provider does. For example, a financial advisor might say, "I'm really glad you have an advisor you are so loyal to. I rarely see advisors perform at that level. I'm sure he calls you at least every three months, creates above market returns with below-market risk, and has decreased your taxes by at least 25 percent. Is that true?"

Unless the prospect is dishonest, they will tell you how their current advisor has fallen short. They will also tell you what they are not getting and what they would like to see in the future. All you have to do then is ask if those shortcomings are important to them. If they say yes, you've now created a wedge.

An even better technique for separating the prospect from their provider is to simply ask questions. You can also start by making an introductory statement and asking about the prospect's situation. Again, never criticize the incumbent. You will never win by telling the prospect how they made a mistake. They have to fire their provider before they decide to meet with you.

Here's a sample script using a financial planning example that you can use to create a wedge.

SALES REP: Our goal is to keep our clients from losing any money. Research from Jeremy Siegel at the Wharton School of business has shown that for every 20 percent loss, you must get a return of 40 percent just to break even. Tell me about your investment returns over the last ten years. Did you take any losses?

PROSPECT: Well, yeah, I did. But didn't everybody?

SALES REP: Actually, not one of our clients lost a penny. I'm sure that was also the case with you, right?

PROSPECT: I wasn't so lucky. I lost 35 percent over the last two years.

SALES REP: So, according to Siegel, it now will take a 70 percent return to get back to even. Are you OK with that?

PROSPECT: No. I'm very irritated. I can't believe that I made such big mistakes.

SALES REP: Well, it's not your fault. I am sure your advisor did the best he could to get the best returns possible. I'm sure he called you at least once a week to present options. He probably also diversified your account so that all your eggs weren't in one basket, mitigating losses, right?

PROSPECT: No. I wish he had done that.

SALES REP: What would you like me to do?

PROSPECT: I just don't want to lose any more money.

SALES REP: If we could make sure you don't lose another penny, keep in close contact, and always keep you in the loop, would that be a better way to go?

Through this questioning process, you are not attacking their strategy or relationship. You are not blaming their financial mistakes on the provider, and you're definitely not pitching. But through this questioning process, you are first creating a wedge between them and their advisor. Only then can you present solutions that will cause them to work with you.

Avoid Being the Same

It's critical to differentiate yourself from their current provider. If all they get is what they currently have, they won't move. But if you can listen first to what they want and then show how you are better in those areas, a wedge is created. If you try to match strengths, you lose. But if you find out the incumbent's weaknesses and present your strengths, you've taken the first step to winning the sale. If you want to buy a car and every dealership has the exact color and style, you'll always go for the cheapest price. Yet that is often how you sell: you present exactly what people have and expect them to do business with you. Or you present what their current provider is doing and expect them to move. That will not make them change.

The Latent Wedge

It is often been said that you need to find pain in order to administer a cure. The pain may have been there all along, but it may be latent. You just have to get the prospect to tell you what it is. During one speech of mine, I had an attendee stand up and said,

"Your prospects probably just tell you when they want to buy. They just hold her hand up in the middle of the interview and say, 'Stop talking, I'm ready, close me!'" Then I looked at the attendee and said, "That happens to you, right?"

He looked at me, and I said, "Me neither!"

All I really had to do was present a perfect scenario and challenge the attendee to be honest. This created a need I could sell to.

An example of the latent wedge is to find a need that has been there all along. For example, we know clients want to be contacted every few months by their financial advisors. The average producer only contacts their A-level clients about once a year, if at all. It's simply not worth it to provide stellar service to those who pay for economy. But this is the latent need you can exploit. One way to say this is, "A lot of my clients really want contact with their advisor every few months instead of once a year. Is this something you also want?"

Another way of using the latent wedge is fees. For example, "Many of our clients paid twice as much with other advisors before they came to us. Do you think that ever happened to you?" It is rare for somebody who is neglected who doesn't believe fees or costs are too high. Just listen to the response and create a wedge.

Preserving the Separation

Once you've created a wedge between a prospect and their current provider, you have to prepare the prospect for the incumbent's call. You have to expect the incumbent to preserve their business.

They will ask the client why they are leaving and suggest problems and issues the client hasn't considered.

For example, a financial advisor will say, "The only way anybody can get you better returns is to increase the beta risk. This will create much more volatility and a lot more stress in your portfolio."

Since the client does not know what a beta risk is and doesn't want more volatility, they may become unsure of their decision and reluctant to change. It's up to you to inoculate the client by coaching them on what the incumbent will say when they call to preserve business. Here's one way to do this:

SALES REP: I'm glad that we have found some areas we can help. But there's one more step. Your advisor is going to lose a lot of money in commissions and fees if you leave. He is likely to try as hard as he can to keep your accounts. He will offer the same service and the same plan, even though he hasn't done this all the years you have been with him. What will you say?

PROSPECT: It depends on what he presents.

SALES REP: I can tell you what he is going to say. He will offer the same products and services and try to improve the relationship. The improved service will last for short time, but it will revert back to the service you are getting now. *When somebody has already shown you who they are, you should believe them.* How are you going to respond?

PROSPECT: I'm not going to allow more of the same. I won't let him do that.

SALES REP: Let me tell you a story about one my clients who had an advisor like yours (insert story here). Do you know what to say to him now?

PROSPECT: I know exactly what to say.

If you can coach your prospects on the responses the incumbent is likely to give and prepare them for the attempt he will use to conserve the relationship, you will insert a wedge between them and the existing provider.

6

Getting Referrals from Partners (Centers of Influence)

There are several sources of referrals:

    1. **Proactive referrals.** These are the names you get when you ask for introductions. Ask for them on a frequent basis.

2. **Advocacy referrals.** Keep in contact with your A and B clients every few months. They will talk about you to their friends, colleagues, and family. When they refer to you in a conversation, their network is much more likely to call you first instead of scouring for somebody else.

3. **Centers of influence (COIs).** These individuals (in some industries we call them *specifiers*) will refer business to you because a client or customer has shown a need. Often these COIs know several people like you to whom they can refer business. But it's a matter of, "Out of sight, out of mind." The more they hear from you, the more referrals you'll get. The less you contact them, the more they will refer business to your competition.

One of my tennis friends, Phil, is a high-level CPA. He works for only about ten corporations and is highly compensated. I fired my corporate accounting firm and searched for a new provider. After a tennis match, I asked Phil if he would be willing to do my taxes and give me planning advice. He was very polite but said he would be too expensive for a small firm like mine. He recommended another of our tennis friends, Nancy, an enrolled agent (EA), who did taxes for smaller corporations. There are many EAs in our area looking for new business. I could have done a search in Southern California and had my pick of providers. But Phil was a center of influence and suggested someone who was well respected and would do a great job.

Why Nancy? She is good at what she does. But many EAs are good at what they do. Frequency of contact made Phil think of her first. It helped that I knew her as well, but anybody Phil recommended would have been a good choice for me.

That's the benefit of COIs. If you are a realtor, your COI could be a mortgage broker, title company, real estate appraiser, attorney, or accountant. If you are an insurance agent or financial advisor, your COI could be an estate planning attorney, accountant, real estate agent, or even a property and casualty agent. (Just make sure the P&C agent does not do life insurance or financial planning.) If your specialty is car sales, your COIs would be auto repair shops and property and casualty agents, as well as auto parts stores. The connections are endless, but your network has to be solid. The most important concept in using COIs is frequency of contact. Those who contact their specifiers most frequently will get the highest number of referrals.

When I speak at mortgage conferences, there are always real estate companies manning the booths. When I speak to real estate conferences, mortgage, appraisal, and title companies are always among the exhibitors. The most important thing is not to just exhibit a couple of times a year at conferences or mail a newsletter once a month. These are great branding exercises, but they don't make sales. Production comes from telephone or face-to-face contact. Your business will be built by frequency of contact.

Below are some COI ideas that will build your business. Most importantly, you will learn specific steps in working with the people who are most likely to refer business to you. You will learn what they want, what they need, their biggest worries, and how to attract these clients to you. You will learn the most elegant ways of making and staying in contact.

Some of the best ways of finding COIs are the providers your clients and customers already use. Instead of making cold calls to get attention, you really should be contacting your best clients and asking who their advisors are. When you call a COI and let them know that you both share a client, they will be very interested in talking, at least out of respect for the client. In those rare cases where a COI is unwilling to talk, make it very plain that you will tell the client about how resistant the COI is. But that will happen very infrequently. Asking clients for the names of their vendors will pave the way for wonderful COI relationships.

CPAs and Attorneys

Many top sales pros mention CPA referrals as among the easiest to sell and the most affluent business they get. Yet getting a CPA, or any other accountant with a client base, to make a referral to you is often difficult. There are many reasons for their reluctance. Often they believe there's no benefit, only a downside, to mentioning you as a resource.

Many years ago, my CPA, John Kearns, said that if I ever had a limited partnership that needed an evaluation, he was my guy. He would let me know the risks, whether it was a good investment, and if it was worth the money. I brought the first partnership to him, which was rejected. He explained that the holding period was too long, there were no guarantees of returns, and the tax implications were sketchy.

A week later, I brought another limited partnership to him. He again gave me three good reasons why it had problems. After a third rejection, I asked him what kind of partnership he would approve. John said, "To tell you the truth, there is not a single partnership that would make me put my neck on the line. If it works, it's good for you. If it blows up, I get the blame. I might as well not endorse anything rather than get the blame in case anything goes wrong." At $1,500 per evaluation, I spent $4,500 to learn that he wouldn't approve anything. This is the way that CPAs, EAs, and other accountants think. The same can be said for their attitude toward referrals.

The biggest reason accountants are reluctant to refer is fear of losing the client. Attorneys often feel the same way, as do many other professional specifiers or recommenders. Attorneys are likely to refer clients, yet only 33 percent of these will end up booking appointments with you. Attorneys especially feel the pressure to avoid risk. They often see only a downside. Because they are trained to see risk, they see danger behind every tree.

When I went through my divorce in 1988, my attorney recommended that I hire a psychologist who could testify in court about whether or not I was a good father. I asked which shrink she would recommend. She said it was my decision. When I pressed her, she gave me a sheet of about five that could be good. I developed a friendship with another father, who was a fellow client. He recommended one he used from the list and said that our attorney always uses the same one. Why couldn't she have told me that in the first place? This is an example of why it's so difficult to get attorneys to make specific recommendations. Their mindset is that they don't want it to be their fault if the referral doesn't work out.

This makes sense. Sixty-two percent of CPA referrals become clients because CPAs only recommend one provider. Attorney referrals end up using recommended providers because they introduce their clients to at least three providers to mitigate their risk of a referral going bad.

Attorneys are even more risk-averse and are very reluctant to make any referral recommendations at all. In response, attorneys often recommend three possible choices, while CPAs recommend only one.

Since CPAs and attorneys, as well as many other COIs, are usually not very good salespeople themselves, they often don't value the power of referrals. Often they have so many sales producers like you chasing them that they really don't have to develop network relationships. They know that referrals will just naturally come to them. One of my clients contacted a CPA and asked to develop a relationship. The accountant was very happy to say yes. After six months, my client realized it was a one-way street. The CPA had been given twenty referrals, while my client received zero. When asked why the CPA didn't reciprocate, he said, "I really don't have to refer business to others. I know that people like you will always give me a steady stream of referrals."

That's the kind of mindset you will have to deal with. CPAs know they have something of a monopoly. No matter what they do, they will get business in the door. You have to be especially effective in making sure CPAs, attorneys, or any other referral sources know that you can help them hit their goals. But first you have to know what those goals are.

Outline of a Typical CPA Practice

The first important thing to know about getting accountants to refer business to you is how their practice works. Nearly every producer like you asks to develop a referral relationship. The accountant will always say yes and will rarely reciprocate. But if you understand their practice and their goals, you will build value in the relationship, and they will be much more willing to reciprocate.

1. Many accountants have more than a thousand clients.

Any compliance-based business will naturally have a lot of clients. Unfortunately, when someone is forced to use an advisor, they often look for the cheapest one. That is why tax companies like H&R Block, Liberty, Triple Check, and many others compete over cheap tax returns. Like your practice, they often have A- and B-level clients. Many national tax companies never keep in contact with their annual clients. They only see clients at tax time and rarely talk in between. They may mail a newsletter, but rarely do they ever make a phone call or see the client face-to-face except during tax time. You want to stay away from the national firms and instead focus on small accountant tax practices, which are likely to maintain a relationship with clients.

2. **Ten percent of an accountant's clients are affluent and will pay more than $10,000 in fees per year.** These are often business clients. The reason for these high fees is that CPAs often do more than just tax returns: often they also do management accounting, tax planning, and corporate audits. They are frequently looking for more of these kinds of clients, but don't know how to find them.

As I've mentioned, when I spoke at a conference of American Institute of Certified Public Accountants (AICPA), I had to change my topic from "Sales Magic" to "How to Read Your Client's Mind." The CPAs couldn't bear seeing the word "sales" in a title and would most likely not have attended the meeting. The corporate accounting people stared at me during the whole speech, as if people skills was a foreign concept to them. The CPAs in private practice were mildly interested, although not enough to take notes.

At one point during the speech, I asked the group how many were actively looking to build their practice. Only one or two hands went up out of five hundred. I then saw one middle-aged guy in the second row respond to my question, "Do you want your practice to grow?"

He smiled and said, "I guess. Doesn't everybody?"

I then asked what he was doing.

He said, "Word of mouth," he said.

I asked what that meant. Predictably, he didn't know. It was just something he'd heard before. The upshot is that accountants in private practice want to grow their business and hit their goals, but they don't know how.

3. **The largest percentage of an accountant's revenue occurs in the first 5.5 months of the year, followed by a severe dropoff.** Accountants are very good at sending out notices in November, trying to get clients to do their taxes early. But there's a severe income drop around April 15 as the deadline approaches. If you ask to engage in a referral conversation with a CPA from March 1 until April 15, they will probably push back. From May until Christmas, they have nothing but time. The only exceptions are those who work on corporate tax returns in October. Most of these people would rather have consistent activity and income throughout the year rather than working eighteen-hour days for three months.

Five Reasons Why CPAs Don't Refer

1. **They are afraid of losing their client if the referral goes wrong.** As I've mentioned earlier, CPAs are perfectly willing to take your

money for evaluating an investment product, but will rarely put their name behind endorsing it because of the risk. The same thing is true with referrals. If the referral goes bad, it's their fault, and they will lose a client.

2. **They simply don't know how to make the referral effectively.** They may see losses but don't recognize how to prevent them in the future. They only know how to capture losses on current or past tax returns. CPAs, EAs, and other accountants can look at a tax return and only see history. They are very inclined to recommend a tax loss carryforward to decrease taxes on profits in the future. They are also very good about what to do when they see investment losses, but they are very bad at spotting poorly performing assets or recognizing a bad retirement investment. They are not trained to spot whether an investment will run out of money in the future or is too volatile to be of value in a retirement plan. They can tell you what tax bracket you are in but won't even think about how much tax you might have to pay five years from now.

Fifteen years ago, I recognized that my defined benefit pension plan was not performing well. I called my CPA and asked for his recommendation. He referred me to a pension plan actuary, who also was noncommittal. He was only trying to make sure my plan was organized correctly. He had no idea how it would perform in the future. Finally, I asked the actuary what he would do in my position. Finally, after pulling teeth, he said he would freeze the plan and transfer the assets to individual IRAs for my staff and me. This was a very simple fix, which I had thought of months earlier. But why my CPA or pension plan actuary could not have been more forward-thinking is beyond me.

In any event, that is how a financial advisor can expect an accountant to behave and think. You can't expect them to recommend you very often, except when the client asks for investment help or in an area you specialize in. But you can be top of mind.

3. **They don't know how to describe you.** They don't know what differentiates you from others. Have you ever heard an accountant refer another professional to their client? It goes like this, "I know a financial advisor that might be able to help you. You should give them a call. Here's his phone number." They won't say much about you or what you are an expert at.

We discussed elevator speeches earlier. Since either you did not tell the accountant your elevator speech or they didn't remember it, you will be described as a generic provider instead of a unique, special, and talented professional. If you didn't do a very good elevator speech and the accountant doesn't know your brand, you will become a commodity. On the other hand, if he or she describes you as unique and valuable, you will not only be treated as a sought-after professional but will also be able to charge higher fees and prices.

In other words, does the CPA describe you as a financial advisor? Or does he describe you as a retirement advisor who is able to ensure that your portfolio has a lot let less risk and is built to provide a stream of income until you pass? There's a difference between the two. One is somebody that you might call someday. The other is someone you will drive a few hours to see. It's all in the way the referral source describes you.

I see an integrative medicine physician who is a ten-minute drive away from my home. I was shocked to learn that her patients fly from all over the United States to consult her. What makes her special is her background: she is not only an MD but has also worked as a chemist and started as an Army physician before private practice. Would you fly five hours to see a physician? Probably not. Would you fly five hours to see someone who could add ten years to your life? Undoubtably.

This is partly why it's critical to keep in contact with an accountant COI on a frequent basis. You should call them every three months, at least to remind them of what you do. Tell stories, as we described earlier. Keep talking about how you help your clients. Eventually it will get through and stay in their memory. You have to nail down your elevator speech. You have to label yourself, memorize the three things you do for your clients better than anybody on earth, and have a story you can tell persuasively even if someone wakes you up at three o'clock in the morning. Also, don't forget the takeaway: "I'm not sure all this will help you, but I would love to hear more about you first."

4. **They think of you like other brokers and advisors.** Their first thought is that you are a producer who thinks about making a commission first. The client relationship is a secondary thought.

CPAs and other accountants are especially wary of those who make money from commissions. An accountant's income is based on fees. They trust providers who earn money the same way. If you are a commission-based realtor, an insurance agent, or other vendor, make sure you make a special point of telling the

CPA how you put the client's needs first, before your own commissions. For example, tell them how you directed a client to another professional even though it meant a loss of income for you. In other words, you did what was right for the client. This will go a long way toward encouraging the CPA to refer more business.

Allay the CPA's fear of losing the client by telling them that the client's best interest comes first, before you make any money.

You can make the CPA or attorney feel more comfortable about losing clients by tell them a story about how you gave up a fee or commission in order to better serve the client. Prove through a story that the CPA or any COI's client interests come first before you make any fees. Tell stories illustrating your fiduciary focus on putting clients first.

5. **They often say that they already know two or three brokers.** Often an accountant will tell you that they already have a relationship with people who do what you do. This is a reflex response. It's the first thing that pops out of their mouth when you ask about a referral relationship. I'm sure they know two or three people who do what you do, but that doesn't mean they are making referrals to these people. They provide very few referrals to anybody, for the reasons discussed earlier. Furthermore, other providers are probably not keeping in enough contact to be at the top of the accountant's mind. Just push back at this response and talk more about the accountant's goals and needs. Do not be put off.

Three Products CPAs Offer

1. **Tax returns.** This is the bread and butter of a typical accounting practice. Up to 80 percent of their income is from tax returns, and that income stream stops on tax day, about April 15.

2. **Tax and estate planning.** Every accountant would like more tax planning and financial planning work. I have spoken at conventions and consulted to many companies that train CPAs to become financial advisors because of their amazing client base. Moreover, CPAs are inherently trusted by their clients. But these financial planning–based CPAs are still relatively rare. They are often looked down by tax-only CPAs, who think that making commissions is very down-market. Most have very poor sales skills and often just present solutions to clients without much listening.

3. **Miscellaneous (forensic accounting, corporate audits, bookkeeping, and financial planning).** CPAs rarely recommend individual investments, just asset classes. They may discuss investments from a tax basis but often don't do wealth or retirement planning. Even the CPAs who do financial planning are unable to do much more than recommend investment vehicles. Rarely do they have the skills to engage in long-term retirement or generational planning that leaves money or protects heirs.

Some accountants are able to do forensic work for the government and even for attorneys. They are rare too.

My divorce attorney in 1988 used a forensic accountant who was specially trained to look for hidden assets and project income from tax returns. His skill set was valuable and unique. He also happened to be my attorney's husband. Many CPAs would love to have that income stream but don't have the sales skills to capture these opportunities.

CPAs often have the same goals as you. The key goals of a CPA are:

1. They want to grow their practice through service offerings, but don't know how to sell them.
2. They want to retain clients, but they don't have any systems that creates loyalty.
3. They want more affluent clients, yet don't want any lower-level tax return work.

How to Get High-Quality Referrals from CPAs

Get CPAs from your clients. It is better to market to a lot of CPAs than to be rejected by a few and stop. Never depend only on one CPA to give you referrals. Whenever you meet with a new prospect or an existing client, ask who their CPA or accountant is. Let the client know that the CPA could be better informed if they knew what you were doing with them as well.

At some point, call the CPA and let them know that you share a common client. They will be more than happy to meet and discuss your mutual client. At that point you can also mention what you do and how it will benefit their other clients.

Ask a new prospect who their CPA is during the fact-finding process. They will be happy to give you a name. A much more efficacious way is to ask a current client who their accountant is during one of your three-month phone calls. As you recall, calling your clients every three months to do an update is critical in building advocacy referrals.

Again, after you do the update, search for needs using the five-step bridge. If you can't find any needs, substitute the CPA request for the referral. It's virtually the same conversation. The way to ask is, "By the way, I would love to learn the name of your accountant. I want to discuss the kinds of things we've done together. It will help streamline their work and will also give them an idea of what we are doing together. Do you mind giving me their name and contact information? Do you have a relationship with them? Do they keep in contact with you?"

If your client uses a different tax firm every year, don't ask for a referral: there is no relationship. But if they know the name of their accountant, even though they only talk during tax season, there may be an opportunity for COI referrals. If you already have the name of their CPA, ask if they have an estate planning attorney. While you're at it, find out if they have a realtor, mortgage broker, or any other advisor whom you could make into a referral partner.

As a realtor, you could ask about their CPA at the end of a three-month phone call. You could also ask about their mortgage broker, appraiser, or any other professional with whom they have a relationship. As we discussed before, the best way to get referrals is to listen. Your clients will almost always mention the names of people they know. You can guide the conversation toward any direction. You don't have to ask for the name of their CPA directly. Instead you can ask about taxes and migrate the conversation towards who they use. These are always very simple, elegant conversations.

Call the COI. If you call the CPA, accountant, or any other center of influence, use our referred lead script, as discussed earlier. Introduce yourself, name your company and your common client, and engage. For example, "Hi, Mr. Smith, my name is Kerry Johnson with Johnson Financial. We have a mutual client named Mary Thompson. You know Mary, don't you?"

Also use voicemail in the way discussed earlier. Mention your name, company, mutual client, and ask them to call you back. For example, "Hi, Mr. Smith, my name is Kerry Johnson with Johnson financial. Please call me back regarding Mary Thompson. My telephone number is xxx-xxx-xxxx."

If the CPA values the client, you'll receive a call back fairly quickly. If you did not get one after three tries, use the three-call script we have discussed earlier. After three calls without any success, let the client know that their accountant, or any other COI, is unwilling to call back. It's assertive, but it will work.

When You Get Them on the Phone

1. **Introduce yourself.** Mention who you are, name your company and referral source, and engage. Like any other referral, the CPA will say something about your mutual client, perhaps how long they've known each other.

2. **Elevator speech.** Ask if the client has said anything about you. Then do your elevator speech as discussed earlier. The steps are:

3. **Label yourself.** Tell them three benefits you provide better than any of your competition.

4. **Tell them a story.** Preferably about how conservative you are in helping your clients and that you always put clients first, before your fees and commissions.

5. **Transition to what you are currently doing for your mutual client.** This is a very simple conversation in which you talk about the client's retirement goals and your strategy for them. You could talk about their risk tolerance and why you have them positioned in safe investments. You can also talk about any alternative investments that might be appropriate. Above all, tell the CPA what you are doing for the client and why you are doing it.

A realtor would have a similar conversation but would talk about why the client sold their last property and their future goals. Or talk about what they're hoping to buy in the future and why. If you're a mortgage broker or any other service provider, you can figure out a similar script.

The whole purpose of this conversation is to get the accountant to engage so that you can gracefully segue to a conversation about their business. If possible, book a face-to-face appointment. Make a phone call a last resort. Face-to-face will generate a lot more opportunities for you.

Use Bridging Steps to Find Out about Their Practice

Here are the steps for using the bridging process to find out about the accountant's practice:

1. **Introductory sentence.** Ask about their business. Ask about the kind of clients they have and how long they've been doing it. Ask about their goals and what they are doing to reach them.

2. **Search for needs.** We know that CPAs generally want to increase their top-level clients. They want more nontax work, like corporate accounting, audit, forensic accounting, and other services that will produce revenue between May and December. Simply ask them about these other services and what they are doing to develop this business. They will say "word of mouth" nearly every time. This simply means they are doing nothing to develop business and are unconsciously waiting for the phone to ring.

3. **Recap needs.** Since you have mastered the five-step bridge, you know how to recap the needs you've discovered. Just in case you need a refresher, here's a sample conversation.

"So if I've heard you correctly, you said you would love to get more top-level tax clients, more ancillary services during the off-season, and a strategy to keep your best clients from leaving in the future. Did I get that right?" Because you listened and didn't pitch, they will agree or even add to how they described their needs and goals.

4. **Trial close.** You have also mastered the trial close. You have learned never to pitch. You now only listen for needs. You also know how to commit people to finding solutions to their goals instead of asking if they want to buy. The same strategy you learned earlier is useful now. For example, "If we could talk about how to get more top-level tax clients, more ancillary services during the off-season, and a strategy to keep your best clients from leaving in the future, would that be helpful?"

Since they've already told you what they wanted, you will gain agreement every time. At this point you've developed a solid center of influence. You've listened to their goals. You've qualified whether they are somebody you would like to work with. And finally, you have committed them to allowing you to help them hit their goals.

If the Center of Influence Won't Talk

Sometimes CPAs and other centers of influence won't talk to you about their practice. You may not have enough rapport, or they may not trust you enough to be candid. Suggest what other CPAs are doing to build the practice. For example, "Often CPAs I speak to increase their top-level clients, develop their ancillary services in the off-season, and retain their best clients. Is that the case with you? What are you doing right now to achieve these goals?" At this point, just listen.

There are many directions you can go in if you know the needs of the CPA or any other center of influence. You can suggest a seminar, inviting their top clients as well as inviting yours. You can offer a special discount or service only available to their clients. You can be very creative.

When the COI Is a One-Way Street

Often a CPA, attorney, or any other specifier is unwilling to refer business but expects you to give them new clients. About 90 percent of my coaching clients have a center of influence relationship, but only 10 percent get referrals back from their specifiers.

It may seem heavy-handed, but it's critical for you to lay out the relationship from the beginning in an elegant way. For example, you might say, "I would love to refer my clients to you. You seem at the top of your game and would a great benefit to my clients. A few years ago, another CPA accepted more than twenty referrals without reciprocating at all. It was a one-way relationship. I'm sure you would never do that, would you?" This is an elegant way of delivering a veiled threat. Instead you are able to directly display your expectations of the relationship. I promise the center of influence will get it.

Getting Mass Referrals from COIs

Since CPAs and other specifiers often have poor sales skills and can't remember enough about you to make a recommendation, they may not refer as many clients as you would like. To solve this problem, ask about their top-level clients. Have they ever held events for them? Do they ever get clients together for appreciation meetings? Do they do more than just provide services?

Offer to speak at a CPA's client event. You can even suggest a small affair like a wine tasting, or even a lunch with a small group of clients. Personally, I would pay for the whole thing. You will get at least 50 percent of the attendees to book appointments with you. It is certainly worth the cost. To make it even more enticing for the center of influence, offer to invite your top clients as well. The only caveat is to not invite clients who already have a CPA relationship that you may be trying to capture. You don't want to kill your existing referral sources.

Since most CPAs have never done a client event, you may have to lay out what they can expect. Generally, 65 percent of the attendees will either book an appointment or display an interest in using the center of influence in the future. Let's assume that my estimate is way too high. Let's say that 40–65 percent of the attendees will probably be interested in using the CPA's services. Only the most callous and uninterested CPAs would not jump at that.

Think about how many centers of influence it would take to make you wealthy. Let's assume the average CPA has one hundred top clients. Our research has shown this is probable. Let's also assume that half of these clients will come to an event both you and the CPA speak at. If you do three events with fifty of the CPA's clients in attendance, you will gain approximately eighty new clients. You can do the math on what one client is worth in commissions and fees, but my guess is that a single CPA event could be a few years' worth of business. What would it be like if you had a couple of these relationships?

Sometimes CPAs and other specifiers are skeptical about having someone speak to their clients. There is a risk, and COIs don't like risk. To make them feel better, give them a video of one of your speeches. If you don't have any presentations recorded, give them a PowerPoint copy of a presentation to make them feel comfortable with the content.

Only about 10 percent of the CPA's client base is affluent enough to be of value to you. Yet CPAs also want new referrals and want to keep the loyalty of the clients they have. Again, research has shown that having one product that a client uses engenders a 36 percent loyalty rate over five years. Two products engender a 56 percent rate, and three or more products create client retention at a whopping 92 percent. Yet CPAs usually only offer two products: tax planning and tax returns. If a client works with you through financial planning, it will allow the CPA to gain more client loyalty, building more products loosely linked to the CPA's, since they control the relationship.

Getting Clients to Attend an Event

A big challenge is to get the CPA to market an event. Since they don't know how to sell, they will be very uncomfortable marketing an event. Even the simplest marketing is often intimidating. All they really have to do is send an invitation out to their top-level clients and follow up with a phone call, but I personally would never depend on them to do even this.

Offer to send the invitation out to their clients and ask if you can follow up with a phone call. A personal call will generate about a 25 percent greater response rate. The CPA probably won't put in the effort, mainly because they feel uncomfortable doing any marketing. Be assertive in asking. Obviously you want to present the seminar in an elegant way.

In the invitation, ask the client to bring a friend. Create a sexy retirement topic like, "The Seven Mistakes Retirees Make." Hold the meeting at a high-class restaurant or country club. You might even want to offer a drawing and grand prize to those who bring a friend. Let the CPA speak first for five to ten minutes about tax law changes. If you are a financial advisor, speak for another thirty to forty-five minutes about a retirement planning concept. A realtor could talk about home values and what the future could bring, how to market a home successfully, or how to buy properties effectively. A mortgage broker could talk about rates and how the economy affects home values.

When COIs Don't Want to Build Their Business

Some CPAs don't care all that much about increasing their business. One of our clients, Jack, spoke to a CPA at a regional firm. The CPA said that the company grows by acquisitions instead of referrals, but also said that they use an advisory firm to do financial planning for their clients. Jack asked if the firm did Social Security planning for clients. The CPA said no. Jack asked if the CPA had Social Security services as part of the firm. Again no. Jack asked if the CPA thought it was important to offer that kind of planning. The CPA said, "Of course" and on the spot offered referrals to five clients who needed Jack's advice.

That same scenario repeated with a small CPA, who didn't want to grow their practice either, but did want to help clients with

Social Security planning. In each case, Jack offered to do a special seminar for any clients over sixty years of age who may want to learn more about Social Security and plan better for it.

This single Social Security innovation has turned CPAs who don't care about building their practice into ones that care about helping their clients who are near retirement to prepare. When you use the bridging technique and discover a CPA who doesn't want to grow their practice, offer other services instead. As Jack's experience shows, you can build a lot of great referrals.

Expected Results from Client Events

If you call potential attendees the days after the invitation hits, 65 percent of them will attend. Of these, 65 percent will bring guests if asked. Sixty-five percent of both clients and guests will book appointments with you. You can do the math. It's definitely worth paying for the whole evening if you get any pushback from the CPA about cost.

Since the CPA will often be nervous about losing clients, try to record your next retirement seminar presentation and give it to the CPA. It will likely calm them down and make them more confident in conducting an event with you.

Jeff, one of my coaching clients in Ohio, developed a relationship with CPA named Tina. At first Tina was skeptical about sponsoring an event. Jeff gave her a forty-five-minute recorded speech from a past retirement planning seminar. Tina became more confident when she had an idea of what he would say. She agreed to the event and gave Jeff the names of potential attendees. Jeff sent the invitations, and Tina hired a temp to make the phone calls, who was paid by Jeff. Out of fifty clients invited, thirty attended and brought about fifteen guests. Tina spoke at the meeting for ten minutes about tax law changes and deductions. Jeff spoke for forty-five minutes about how to create a safe retirement. He booked appointments with twenty of the clients and eight guests. Tina also booked appointments with ten guests.

My client Kevin in Arizona holds CPA client meetings on a monthly basis. The CPAs make so much money from the meetings that they usually pay Kevin for the expenses. This approach is definitely thinking outside the box for CPAs, but when they finally get it, they will be committed to working more and more with you.

While CPA client events are not the only way of gaining new prospects, they are one of the best methods for gaining more affluent clients with minimal expense. Since CPAs are not very sales savvy, simply offering this seminar will not be enough. As with the 65 percent rule in seminar events, 65 percent of the CPAs will be keen on doing a seminar. Keep passing on seminar results to them as you collect experiences with other CPAs. They will undoubtedly follow the rest of the herd.

How to Present to a COI

Here's an example of how Bob, one of my clients, was able to use CPA referral techniques. He called a CPA to book an appointment.

BOB: You and I have a mutual client named John Smith. John said great things about you. He also said you are a scratch golfer. Congratulations! I would love to chat with you about some of the financial planning that I have done with John. Can we meet for lunch next Thursday at noon?

At the CPA's office, they spoke for twenty minutes about the financial planning he had done with their mutual client. The CPA mentioned that he wished every financial advisor could give him an update. This would help his tax preparation go much more smoothly.

BOB: I would love to talk to you for a few minutes about a survey I just read from my business coach, Dr. Kerry Johnson. He was the keynote speaker a few years ago at the AICPA national convention. He said the typical CPA practice has about one thousand clients. About 10 percent of the practice is the most profitable and generates about $10,000 per year in fees and income per client. He also said the largest percentage of a CPA's income occurs before June 1. Is that true with you?

CPA: Yes, except the top 10 percent of my affluent clients contribute a little bit less: $8,000 per year.

BOB: Dr. Johnson also mentioned that CPAs have three ways of gaining business: tax returns, which make up about 75 percent of their income; tax planning, which accounts for about another 20 percent; and broad-based financial planning, forensic accounting, and corporate audit work, which account for the rest. The study also showed that most CPA firms want more affluent clients but don't have a system for getting them. Often they gain more low-level tax return work than the high-level, affluent, corporate work from which they make the most money. The last thing the study showed was that if you have one product or service, there is only a 32 percent chance of client retention over five years. If you offer two services, there is a 52 percent chance, and three or more services equals a 92 percent chance of retention over five years. Is all this true in your practice?

CPA: Yes, that's right on the money

BOB: Tell me, how do you let people know about the other services you offer besides tax returns?

CPA: Just word of mouth.

BOB: Well, it seems that if you had a systematic way of letting people know about your other services, your income would go up. Correct?

CPA: I guess so.

BOB: What is your system for getting more affluent clients?

CPA: No real system, just word of mouth.

BOB: What system do you have for client retention?

CPA: Again, just word of mouth.

BOB: So what I'm hearing you say is that you have no system of gaining new affluent clients or retaining current ones, and you don't have any real way of letting clients know about your other services. Did I get that right?

CPA: I guess so.

BOB: So if we could focus on helping you gain more affluent clients, appropriately sell more of your services, and increase affluent client retention over five years, would that help?

CPA: Absolutely.

Bob: One way of accomplishing all these things is through a client event. I would love to sponsor a dinner for your clients at Ruth's Chris restaurant. We could also encourage clients to bring their friends by saying that everybody who brings a friend will be entered into a drawing for a free iPad. The more friends they bring, the better their chance of winning. Only invite your A clients if you want to gain more A referrals. I envision you speaking for ten minutes about tax law changes and your other services like tax planning, followed by me speaking for thirty minutes about safe retirement techniques. I predict that 65 percent of your clients will bring their friends, and 65 percent of their friends will book appointments with you. By the way, here are some PowerPoint slides I will discuss during that meeting. Does this sound interesting to you? Do you think this might work to help you gain more affluent clients?

CPA: I love it. When can we schedule this?

7

How Referable Are You?

Would you like to be more referable? Do you currently know your level of referability? Many producers try to get better results by asking more often. Very few have an idea of how referable they really are.

One of my competitors constantly tells audiences they will get more referrals if they are more referable. I presume this means providing better customer service, communicating better, becoming more honest, and listening more effectively. These are all good ideas, but there is no direct relationship between good customer service and building referrals.

Many companies pay hundreds of thousands of dollars creating and distributing surveys to find out what their clients like and dislike. My wife is a flight attendant for American Airlines. The president of the company does a monthly video called "Crew News." A few months ago, he mentioned that their referability score dropped two points, and they were trying to find out why.

Nearly every company surveys your thoughts about the product service experience. Sometimes you will volunteer an opinion about whether you would use their services again. But responses are rare: most people don't want to take the time to let you know how they feel. Fewer than 5 percent of surveys are completed, and even fewer if there is no compensation. But now you have a tool to find out how your clients think about your relationship and how referable you are. It's called the Net Promoter Score (NPS).

The Net Promoter Score

Most surveys are too cumbersome and don't really give you measurements that you can use. Fred Reichheld, a partner at Bain and Company, spent a decade searching for a simple way of measuring why some clients become raving fans and others are merely satisfied and came up with NPS.

Here is how NPS is implemented. First, ask your clients to answer the question: "How likely, on a scale from 1 to 10, are you to recommend us to a friend or colleague?"

Sort the responses into three groups:

Promoters, 9s and 10s

Passives, 7s and 8s

Detractors, 0 through 6.

The percentage of promoters minus detractors is your score. If you have 75 percent promoters and 15 percent detractors, you have an NPS of 60. This means your referability is only 60 percent. As a rule, anything above 50 percent is good, but referrals don't come consistently unless your score is over 75 percent.

One important consideration is to offer this survey only to your A and B clients. These are the clients from whom you most want to get referrals. Your goal is to constantly drive the NPS score up by asking two follow-up questions:

1. Why did you give us that score?
2. How can we raise that score?

For every 10 percent increase you gain in NPS score, net income will also increase by 10 percent. This makes sense. If you gain more advocacy referrals (remember, these are the folks who call in or clients who talk about you to a friend), your closing ratio will be nearly 85 percent. This prevents you from spending inefficient marketing dollars chasing new business.

Below is an example of how NPS is used.

How likely are you to recommend our firm to a friend or colleague? Please circle the number that best represents your view.

Lowest   1   2   3   4   5   6   7   8   9   10   Highest

Why did you give us this rating?
How specifically can we improve your score?

One of my clients sent an NPS rating sheet to his A and B clients. His NPS score was 50. Then he asked, "Why did you give us this rating?" Many clients responded that they only heard from him once a year. When they answered the question, "How specifically can we improve your score?" many asked to be called once every three months.

When he implemented these three-month phone calls, NPS increased, and referrals started flowing in. His NPS score increased to 90 and advocacy (incoming referrals) started to flow in as well. His income increased by 40 percent within six months.

Another one of my clients is a tanning salon in Southern California. Their NPS score was only 40. When customers were asked why they gave that score, the answer was all over the map. Some said the staff was not very personal. Others said the front desk folks didn't seem to care. Others said the price was too high for the service they received. But when asked what they could do to increase the score, one answer stuck out. The customer wrote, "At least say goodbye when I leave the salon." All the other responses regarding lack of attention and worker interest collapsed into a simple "Goodbye, John. See you next time."

The owner made a very simple change. As a customer signed in, the front desk staffer would glance at the sheet and welcome the customer by name. After the hour tanning treatment, the front desk worker would again acknowledge the person by name and say, "Have a great day. When will we see you again?"

Usually customers chat about their schedule but then make a follow-up appointment. In lingering at the store, they would also pick up extra products. This is a very simple example of what NPS can do. The score of 40 became 80 just as a result of calling people by name as they left the salon.

I was very curious about this simple fix. My gym in Southern California stayed open during the Covid-19 lockdown because it was a physical therapy "essential service." Often I was the only person in the place. Leo, the head trainer, has known me for years and always says hello when I come in. Even though he's with other customers, he will stop and say, "Goodbye, Kerry" as I leave. I also noticed that every other trainer in the gym makes a point of doing the same.

When I asked Leo about this practice, he said they learned many years ago that hello was always nice, but saying goodbye has an impact lasting even longer than a greeting. It also motivates customers to renew memberships faster and purchase extra services more quickly.

NPS is not a complicated mathematical equation that only Fortune 500 companies can afford to implement. It is a very simple tool that can measure your referability. Don't be fooled by customers who tell you on the phone or face-to-face that they like working with you. Maybe they're only being polite. I fired my landscape guy recently because he thought his job was to cut the grass instead of making sure the yard is green. I constantly had to tell him which sprinklers to fix and which gopher holes to take care of. I don't expect a lawn care guy to use NPS, but if he did, he would still be my gardener.

Getting a Better Response Rate

How do you get the NPS surveys back? The last thing on any customer's mind is helping you build your business. What's in it for them? The answer is an offer that will grab their attention. You could give them a $25 gift certificate for each survey. You would get a lot of rating sheets back. Although this would be worth it, that could get very expensive. The answer is a drawing. If the prize is valuable enough, the rating sheet return will be high. One of my clients offered a drawing for a free dinner for two at an upscale restaurant. Another did a drawing for an iPad. One of my clients did a drawing for a three-day weekend for two at a popular resort. This is especially interesting, because the hotel was doing a promotion to get more guests. The advertising costs for the drawing perfectly fit their limited marketing budget. The simple drawing for a dinner increased the response rate from 15 percent to 50 percent.

Another important idea is to set a deadline to get the surveys back. An effective deadline is five days from the date you mail them. Research shows that you can double response rates by setting a time limit. Whenever I send an agreement out for a speech, I assign a deadline. When I take on a new coaching client and attach an agreement, a deadline is highlighted in red. Most of my deadlines are arbitrary, but people respond to time limits. If there is no deadline, compliance drops like a rock.

8

Getting Referrals from Social Media

My favorite social media site is LinkedIn. I both love it and hate it. I love it because I can see whom all my clients are connected to. I hate it because I get barraged from "social media experts" trying to connect and offering to provide leads. Their pitch is always more exposure on Facebook, LinkedIn, Twitter, and any other platform they can think of.

I have yet to see a direct measurable response from any of my social media connections alone. Facebook is famous for data analytics. They know how many times you play golf, what you ate for dinner last night, and the cars you drive. They get this information from the groups you're connected to and what you post. The same as true with other social media platforms. It's not rocket science. They target ads according to the context and content of your posts.

What these social media experts don't understand is that their services are best marketed using personal referrals. By trying to connect with those they don't know, closing ratios tend to be about

as effective as those for a cold call. I get at least five LinkedIn solic-
itations to connect every day. Just this last week I got tired of these
mindless offers. I responded with, "Does this really work for you?
You're trying to sell marketing services when all you are doing
is cold-calling without a telephone. Your business would be a lot
more successful if you learn how to use referrals."

In this section, you will learn not only how to contact people
through social media, but also how to develop relationships. Social
media experts have not yet grasped these skills. Facebook allows
you to become "friends." You can join a group. You can "private
message" them and develop somewhat superficial acquaintances.
Twitter allows you to respond and post.

The other social media platforms are pretty much one-way
traffic. I like YouTube, but even this platform only allows you to
push content to followers.

There is a way that you can use social media platforms as an
introduction. One of these platforms will allow you to connect
and develop a telephone or face-to-face relationship that produces
business. It is measurable, predictable, and will produce results.

LinkedIn is the most effective way to find prospects. You can
use it not only to connect but also book appointments. The way
to use social media sites like Linked in, Facebook, and Twitter is
to let others know who you are. There is a lot more to these sites
than putting up a banner or joining a group. You can also make
connections and make sales.

Here are some specific LinkedIn tips to develop a presence,
connect, and make sales. The clear advantage with LinkedIn is
that when you're connected with somebody, you can see all the

people they are connected to as well. If you have Sales Navigator, you have even more options.

As you make three-month phone calls to your best clients, ask if they are on LinkedIn. At least 75 percent will be. They may not post or even check in very often, but that really doesn't matter. Your goal is to connect with the clients and see their connections. As you make three-month phone calls, do the update and the five-step bridge, use LinkedIn to find people connected to your client that you would like to be introduced to.

Let's say your client has five hundred connections. You can search their locations, industries, and years of career experience. As you make your client phone call, be prepared with four names of people you would like to meet. Just mention those connections to your client. Ask who could benefit from working with you. Generally, they will know about 40 percent of their LinkedIn connections. If you suggest four names, you may get two introductions in response.

Social Media Referral Steps: How to Make This Work

1. **Create your home page on LinkedIn.** Include a photo and the profile you would like people to see. Make your LinkedIn page as attractive as your website. In fact, many experts say that a LinkedIn page is viewed more often than your website, so it had better be good. LinkedIn is "paint by numbers." It will direct you to fill in a bio, pictures, graphics, educational history, and even your goals. Remember, don't make people guess who you are and what you do.

Be very direct and plain. This is your elevator speech. I actually put videos on my LinkedIn page so that all potential clients are aware of what I want them to know.

2. **Groups are very important on LinkedIn and Facebook.** Groups allow you to make at least a superficial connection with people. Join any group that captures your interest. But remember, if you want to gain business, don't join a group of your competitors. Join a group that targets the kinds of folks you would like to have as clients. This way you can become an expert resource.

3. **People are more willing to connect on LinkedIn.** Unlike Facebook, those you choose to connect with on LinkedIn will often accept your request. Even today many think they need to build a massive network, like a teenage girl wanting to be popular in high school: "Look how many friends I have!"

4. **The secret sauce.** When you send a connection request, refer to your client or friend in the note. Never offer to connect without mentioning the referral source. It's often helpful to use the personal touch we spoke about earlier. If in the note you can mention something about their kids or their golf game, your chances of connecting will increase.

Once the person accepts your connection, send a message to them. The most effective request is, "I highly value those I connect with on LinkedIn. I would love to find out more about you and what you do. Can we talk for ten minutes on Wednesday, September 5, at 9:40 a.m.?" Eighty-five percent will accept your request.

At that point ask for their phone number and call at the appointed time.

5. **Don't pitch on the call.** Instead use all the referral skills we have discussed previously. Introduce yourself, give the name of your company and referral source, and engage. Use the personal touch. Give the elevator speech. Use the five-step bridge.

I use this process every day. Once someone accepts my connection, I ask to talk for ten minutes on the following Thursday, mentioning that I want to find out more about them and what they do.

Whenever somebody tries to connect with me on LinkedIn, I use the same process. I send a reply to their invitation mentioning that I only connect with people I can talk to for ten minutes. LinkedIn is not a Rolodex; it's a relationship. I always ask if the individual can talk on the following Thursday at 10:40 a.m. for ten minutes; I want to find out more about who they are and what they do.

This is absolutely the most effective referral business generation process I have ever used. Generally, after my elevator speech, I will ask about their business. They usually go on and on about whom they market to and why they're better than the competition. Since I'm listening, I guide the conversation toward whether they have conferences, what they are doing to increase sales, and even what their biggest challenges are. Of these phone calls, 75 percent produce referrals to either a meeting planner or a coaching prospect. Nearly everybody will ask to buy a book. This is a very effective process in producing business. But if you simply click on people to connect with, you will be disappointed. If you connect with those who already know your clients, you will benefit from the power of referral relationships. I have never once been asked by anyone on LinkedIn, or any other platform, to talk to me on the phone or face-to-face. Everybody realizes that relationships are better than Rolodexes, but nobody puts that knowledge into practice.

For more information on what to say when you get a social media connection on the phone, read the section on the five-step bridge in chapter 4.

Another marvelous way to get and market to referrals using LinkedIn is to identify and target whom you want to gain as a client. If you know who your market is and the kinds of folks you want to talk to, do a search on LinkedIn using keywords. For example, you can look up "financial advisor" and/or "retirement annuity." The results will be in the tens of thousands. Then request a connection; 85 percent will accept. Once you connect, ask to talk on the phone for them minutes about who they are and what they do. This process is so effective that you might want to keep it a secret. If your competitors learn this trick, you might lose your advantage.

You don't have to wait for people to contact you. LinkedIn doesn't need to be only a banner advertisement or a website. You can use it to proactively contact those you want to do business with. It is a super referral source. You can just look at your client's connections and filter those you want to meet. You simply suggest people you would like to be introduced to instead of asking whom they know. This process is so new that the novelty alone will help you make more sales.

LinkedIn Contact Script:
When They Ask to Connect

Here's a script you can use when people try to connect with you:

Hi, (name). Thanks for your invitation to connect on Linked In. I get ten invitations per day to connect, but I choose those I can talk to on the phone for ten minutes. For me, LinkedIn is about building relationships, not just collecting names. My only agenda is to find out more about you and what you do. Are you free to talk for ten minutes on Thursday at 10:40 a.m., California time? I look forward to hearing from you.

—Dr. Kerry Johnson

LinkedIn Contact Script:
When We Ask to Connect

Here's a script to use as you try to connect with others.

Hi, (name). We have a mutual friend (give name). (Client's name) says great things about you and that you (add personal touch). I would love to connect with you on LinkedIn.

—Dr. Kerry Johnson

Use this script once they accept your connection. Use this follow-up note when you ask to talk on the phone after you connect.

Hi, (name). Thanks for connecting with me on LinkedIn. (Mutual friend) says great things about you and that you (personal touch). I would love to talk to you for ten minutes on (give date and time). My only agenda is to find out more about you and what you do.　　　　　　　　*—Dr. Kerry Johnson*

When They Don't Respond

Sometimes people initiate a connection but ignore your request to talk. Here's a script for dealing with them.

Hi, (name). Recently you invited me to connect on LinkedIn. I sent a message a few weeks ago but didn't receive a response.

I get ten invitations per day to connect on LinkedIn, but I only connect with those I can talk to on the phone for ten minutes. For me, LinkedIn is not a blind Rolodex; it's about building relationships. I would like to find out more about you and what you do. If you would rather not talk on the phone, let me know. I look forward to hearing from you.

—Dr. Kerry Johnson

9

"Circle of Friends" Client Events

One of the most effective ways of getting referrals is client events. Getting clients together is not only a wonderful way of retaining business but can be a great way to build it. The problem is that most producers will do something like a wine tasting event or an appreciation dinner. The cost is often $50–$100 per person, yet provides minimal sales benefit. The clients love it, and it makes the producer feel good, but it does little else.

One of my coaching clients recently held a client appreciation dinner. He invited fifty of his clients including spouses and guests. I asked if anybody booked appointments, he said, "A few."

Another one of my enterprising coaching clients takes his clients on a three-day cruise every year. All they have to do is to have referred three people who have become clients over the preceding year. Of his one hundred clients, twenty-five usually qualify. About ten are an elite group that refer many more than the minimal number.

This is a marvelous idea to get referrals. One of the best reasons is PR. In every monthly newsletter, he lists a client who has referred someone. He always mentions those who are in the top ten of referrals for the year. This builds a culture of referrals and creates a sense of community among those clients who have introduced others in the past.

I'm an Executive Platinum (EP) with American Airlines. To achieve this status, a flyer needs 100,000 miles and $15,000 in airfare spending. The benefits are free domestic upgrades as well as some minor niceties like one free drink per flight and a better seat, as well as special customer service telephone numbers and boarding priority. It's amazing how many flyers will spend an extra $5,000–$10,000 and fly many more miles to achieve this status. We EPs call it staying on "the island." The attraction of hitting EP level for a marginal benefit is pretty intense.

The same incentive can be used for your clients who refer business to you. You could also broadcast it monthly to your client base. For example, you could show their progress toward the cruise for the year.

The Messina Method

Many years ago, one of my clients, Bob Messina, did monthly dinner seminars for retirement leads. The purpose of the seminars was to book appointments and sell annuities. His average result per seminar was five to ten appointments from a group of twenty to thirty attendees. The problem was a 25 percent cancellation rate.

Like many habits in life, Bob's were hard to break. The restaurant, Five Crowns, was undergoing construction. At first, he needed a new venue. Bob tried Fleming's, a high-end steakhouse. The dinners were very expensive, but the attendance was high. Unfortunately, he booked the same number of appointments as at the cheaper location. After a few months, he tried an Italian restaurant, thinking a lower cost would be beneficial. He booked the same five to ten appointments, but the attendees were less affluent. The cancellation rate remained about 25 percent.

After a few months of mediocrity, Bob said, "If I can't put more appointments on my calendar, I can't afford to keep you as a coach." I've always believed that the best source of new business is old business. New clients are best sourced by current relationships.

We created the Messina seminar method by focusing on A and B clients and leveraging those relationships to build referrals. I was finally able to get Bob to invite a small group of clients to a dinner at an upscale restaurant. The result was nearly $40,000 in commissions from only a $1,750 cost. Here's how he did it:

Bob invited twelve clients, hoping to get 65 percent to come. He sent an invitation, then followed up by telephone. Nine clients agreed to come.

After each client accepted, he offered free door prizes including a flat-screen TV. To enter the drawing, they needed to bring a guest who could benefit from the kind of relationship they had with Bob.

The language he used in talking to clients was very simple. After client accepted the invitation, Bob said, "I would love to open this up to anybody who could benefit from some of the things we've done together. Whom can you think of? We are going to do a drawing for a free iPad. The more people you invite, the better your chance of winning. Just give us a name and contact info, and we will send out the invitation. It would be very nice if you could call them first and let them know an invitation will be coming."

The great benefit of this message is that you still have a referral even if the client does not come.

Some of my clients mention that attendees sometimes bring their grandchildren or less affluent friends, just to be entered in the drawing. The way around this problem is to tell a story about a client who has brought the wrong person: "What's crazy, Mr. Client, is that we did an event like this a few years ago. One of my clients brought a family member who had no way of benefiting from our services. This was attempt to get the door prize. I know you would never do that, but isn't it crazy what people will do to get a free iPad?" This is a way of inoculating clients from bringing kids or anybody else who will be of little benefit to you by attending the seminar.

The results of the first Messina seminar was nine clients, who brought eight guests. In another meeting, eleven clients brought eight guests. In the beginning, we would just ask clients to bring guests without offering a door prize. It was always surprising how few clients would bring people unless they received an incentive. Never underestimate the power of a door prize to build attendance or referrals. The prizes can be a dinner for two at a high-end restaurant, a big-screen TV, or anything in between.

Bob's appointment results were encouraging. Three of the nine clients booked appointments, as did five of the eight guests. One unexpected benefit was clients who had more needs and booked appointments on their own. We planned on guests booking appointments, but we didn't expect so many clients to respond. This was a wonderful benefit. In a second meeting, two of the eleven clients booked appointments, while five of the eight guests did.

I work with a lot with producers in the financial planning and insurance industries. Nearly all of them think they manage all of their clients' assets, but they rarely do. Here is another reason for the three-month phone call: to gather more assets or upsell clients in order to protect their retirement. Client events do much the same thing. When a client hears about a retirement topic at a seminar, they realize they have more assets at risk and want to talk about what else the financial advisor can do.

If you are a mortgage broker, the Messina program could also help. One of my clients in Salt Lake City, Utah, invited all his clients to a special movie screening. He rented a theater. Nearly one hundred people responded. He encouraged clients to bring guests, and almost fifty showed up. We know that homeowners purchase a new house every seven years and refinance every 3.5 years. Twenty of the guests booked appointments to review their existing mortgages; thirty of the clients did the same. From a $2,000 investment, my mortgage coaching client booked fifty appointments and logged thirty new mortgages in the pipeline, netting him $150,000. Realtors can do the same thing. Anybody with a client base will get the same results.

The unique part about the Messina method was the presentation. The first five minutes were devoted to the greeting. The next ten minutes involved an economic update for the benefit of the current clients. The next hour was a standard dinner seminar discussing a safe retirement, avoiding investment losses, decreasing volatility, and reducing the effects of inflation.

At the end of the meeting, the financial advisor visited every attendee, collected evaluation sheets, and chatted about their concerns. He then booked appointments with three clients and five guests.

The average amount of money you will likely spend on a standard dinner seminar is $600 per closed appointment. The amount of money you will spend booking an appointment at a Messina-style client event will be between $25 and $50. It doesn't take a PhD to know that client events are both economical and successful. Dinner seminars are always a good idea. They should not be abandoned. But doing a client event at least once a month will insulate you from a stretch of poor attendance and a dearth of appointments. It will keep your sales production steady.

Using a Guest Speaker

Some of my coaching clients do frequent client appreciation events. Often they decide to mix it up by using guest speakers. A special guest speaker may get more attendees. In 2009, one of my clients in Tennessee thought he wanted to use an outside speaker. He thought his clients were tired of hearing him and asked me to speak about my new book, *Why Smart People Make Dumb Mistakes with Their Money.*

He drew double the attendees of any other seminar. At the end of the event, he passed out an evaluation sheet asking the attendees to self-rate their concerns from 1 to 5. The areas mirrored the five basic retirement worries of every senior.

1. Running out of money
2. Market volatility
3. Taxes
4. Inflation
5. Family legacy or catastrophic illness

My client asked attendees to raise their hands if they marked three or higher for any one of the questions. Ninety percent of the attendees responded. He then asked the group to mark the box that said, "Yes, I would like to book an appointment." Next he encouraged the attendees to circle a possible appointment time and date over the next week. The next step was to call to confirm those booking appointments. During the phone call, he asked about the answers that were marked three or higher. Since the attendees knew why they were attending the appointments, very few postponed and zero canceled.

The Minicircle of Friends Approach

One very effective technique in gaining referrals is the minicircle of friends approach. This method expends very little money for maximum results. You invite a small group of people for lunch or breakfast in order to attend a miniseminar offering a topic like a market update. You might talk about the economy or the stock market. You could talk about real estate market conditions or even mortgage rates. The topic could be anything that could benefit the attendees. The gathering doesn't have to be lunch or breakfast. It can be a coffee meeting for five. Any venue would work as long as your client can bring a small group of people together to listen to your expertise.

Like the three-month phone call, your presentation is merely intended to get the conversation started. The market update is simply to get people talking about their goals, needs, and what they would like to achieve. This method works best when you let your client introduce you and others around the table. Then give your elevator speech followed by a market or economic update.

The next part is the most important. It's a skill set you already learned: the five-step bridge. As people talk, you should ask questions. As you find needs, recap. Before you leave, trial-close. If the attendees tell you they are interested in the next step, you can book an appointment. At that point, you can exchange telephone numbers and follow up.

The benefit of the minicircle of friends lies in minimal preparation and low expense. On average, you should expect one third of the attendees to book appointments with you. Either way, you will gain more context for your three-month phone call. As you recall, the biggest benefit of the three-month call is timing. It's talking to prospects at the right time: when they need you. Calling them every three months will increase your chances of engaging them when they are ready.

In fact, the most basic way of selling the minicircle of friends approach is the three-month phone call. At the end of the conversation and in place of the referral request, you could say, "I really enjoy working with you. Eighty-three percent of your friends and family will be totally dependent on Social Security at some time during their lives. I would love to take you and a few friends out to lunch or breakfast and do a market update. Whom do you know who could benefit from a meeting like this?"

Again, if you've done this the right way, clients will respond with, "Anybody could benefit from this."

Most of my clients who use this approach book at least one minicircle of friends lunch each week, ensuring a constant stream of new referrals. You can expect approximately one out of every three invitees to bring along friends, family, and colleagues. My hope is that you do at least one of these events every week. It will provide a constant source of referrals for you.

The Minicircle of Friends Steps

1. Identify A and B clients who know people you would like to meet.

2. After the three-month phone call, ask if they would be willing to bring two friends to lunch or breakfast. Here's a script you can use:

> I'm not sure you know this, but 83 percent of your friends and family will be totally dependent on Social Security at some time during their lives. The volatility and pressure on retirement savings is more intense now than ever before. I would love to take you and a couple of your friends to lunch or breakfast to talk about (current crisis or event) in the market and how to keep their money safe in the future. Whom do you

know who might like to hear a private briefing on (current event)?

3. Here are some ideas on how you can run the minicircle of friends event. At the meeting use this format:

    a. Talk about the current event or market for ten minutes.

    b. Try to engage each person in the conversation.

    c. Find out their needs using the bridging technique.

    d. Book an appointment at the meeting or make an appointment to talk later.

The Minicircle of Friends Invitation

One of my clients in Costa Mesa, California, has a unique way of inviting guests: he asks his clients for the names of people they would like to invite. He then sends a personal invitation that reads:

Please be my guest at "Lunch with Swan."

As we've worked together, I have shared with you my mission of helping each of my clients implement sound financial strategies so they can sleep well at night.

During the last crisis, 38 percent left their financial advisors. That number increased to 76 percent in December. Today 82 percent of clients are warning their friends and family away from their own advisors because they've lost so much money. Without any sort of unbiased information, many people are scared and will make wrong decisions without help.

Many of your friends are concerned about whether they will have enough money to last throughout their retirement. Some of your friends wonder if their money is safe. Because of the current market meltdown, many of your friends will have to take unnecessary risks to make up for losses.

"A Meal with Swan" is a private event hosted by my wife Deborah and me. I will do a briefing on what has caused this economic crisis, what's likely to happen, and how you and your friends can keep your money safe.

Our meal will be a time for you and two to four couples chosen from your circle of friends to meet at a restaurant of your choice in a casual and informal setting on a date and time that is mutually convenient. Those you invite can be chosen from your circle of friends.

Please let me know in advance whom you will be inviting so that we can send our invitation directly to them.

I look forward to an evening of fine food, friendly fellowship, and some lively discussion!

We'll talk soon to decide on dates, times, and your favorite restaurant!

Cordially, (your name)

The Bring a Name Campaign (BANC)

As we've seen, there are many ways to gain referrals. You can ask directly and deal with the "I don't know anyone" objection. You can keep in contact with clients every three months and ask who could benefit from a relationship with you. You can also hold client events and ask them to invite guests using the Messina referral method. All these are effective. Another very effective technique for gaining new referrals is the bring a name campaign (BANC).

This is also a client event to which you can invite your A and B clients. The difference between other client events and the BANC method is simply to get clients to bring names. Invite them to an event to hear a speaker or to go to a baseball game or even a theater screening. To attend, they have to give you three names of people they would like you to meet. You can either ask them to produce the names before the event or write down the referrals as they enter. This is unlikely to book as many appointments as when the referral actually hears you speak, but you will gain many more names.

Here are some steps you can use to make the BANC method effective.

1. **Send an invitation to your clients.** Let them know that you will have a special guest speaker, including a nice dinner at an upscale restaurant. Dinner is not required: you can also do an evening event with light refreshments. But you will get a higher attendance with a dinner.

2. **Call three days after the invitation arrives, and ask if they can come.** If so, let them know that you will be giving away a free gift. All they have to do to enter is give you the contact information of those they want to bring. The more names they bring, the better chances they have of winning.

3. **Tell the client that you will be contacting the names sometime in the future via email or by telephone.** Also use the inoculation technique to make sure they don't put names down of teenagers or people who could not benefit by working with you. You don't need the names of unqualified people just so the client has a better chance of winning.

4. **If you have a guest speaker, give any client who produces names a prize for entering.** This could be a free book the speaker has written, a drink coupon, or anything else you think might motivate the client to write down referral names.

A Script You Can Use

Hi, John,

I just sent you an invitation for an event we are having on (date) at (venue). Dr. Kerry Johnson is our special guest speaker, and he will be presenting his newest book, Why Smart People Make Dumb Mistakes with Their Money. *He is a best-selling author and is really entertaining. Can you come?*

Great! We are opening this up to anyone else whom you would like to invite and who could benefit. In fact, we will be raffling off a free iPad for those who bring guests. The more people you bring, the better your chances of winning. We will also be giving you a free copy of Dr. Johnson's book Why Smart People Make Dumb Mistakes with Their Money *just for writing down a name.*

Do you know anyone you would like to bring or even someone you would like to introduce us to?

Please let us know as soon as possible whom you would like to invite and give us their contact info, so we can send an invitation. It would also be really helpful if you could give them a phone call and invite them personally. We will send the invite, but a follow-up phone call from you would really be a nice touch. Can you do that?

The people to invite are folks like you who could benefit from the kind of relationship you have with us. Can you believe it? We did an event like this a while ago, and a client brought a teenage grandson, just so he had a better chance of winning the iPad. We only work with people who are over fifty years old. I know you would never do that, but isn't it crazy what people will do to win a raffle?

Great! Just let us know whom you want to invite, and we will send out the invitation. I look forward to seeing you there.

Invitations Others Have Used

Here's a sample invitation by one client who promoted his own BANC event:

We love our clients!
Come join us for an evening of great food and entertainment at the
Clients and Friends Event
Date: Friday, August 29
Time: 6:00 p.m.

Place: Springdale Country Club
608 West Lakewood Drive
Springdale, AR 72764
(Located on Highway 71B, one mile north of the NWA Mall)
Entertainment will be provided by Harold Chilton, accomplished
arranger and musician. You'll be tapping your foot to the classics.
There will be a short update on current financial topics:
• The current debt crisis and its effects on your retirement
• The price of oil and the future
• The presidential candidates and their policies
Warmest regards,
P.S. I'll be in touch with you next week.
P.P.S. Get ready for a GREAT time!

Not every event has to be financial planning, insurance, real estate, or from the mortgage industry.

10

Conclusion

Y ou've learned a lot from this book. You gained the most relevant and prescient information available on how to build your business using referrals. The hardest part about getting referrals is possessing a mindset expecting that they will come. Most producers like you forget to ask. Most have been rejected so many times that they expect rejection. They anticipate that a referral request will meet with resistance.

In the beginning of this book, you learned referrals are critical. Referrals are 35 percent more likely to do business with you and will produce 25 percent more revenue. You also learned to keep in contact with clients every three months. But just making a phone call or seeing a client face-to-face is not enough. You have to provide information of value every time you call. That information should be an update about something that can be of benefit. Otherwise your client or prospect won't answer the phone.

You've learned that 89 percent of your clients care more about the relationship than the fees or commissions they pay. You also learned that clients want three things:

1. They want to understand what they're buying.
2. They want to know that you are constantly watching out for them.
3. They want frequency of contact. This means a phone call every three months, if not more often.

You've also learned there's a difference between proactive and advocacy referrals. You've learned that a proactive referral (people you call) has a 38 percent chance of booking an appointment, whereas an advocacy referral (when they call you) has an 85 percent chance of doing business with you. Advocacy referrals only come from frequency of contact. They aren't attracted by your competence or stellar results. Referrals come because the client often thinks of you. The only way of building advocacy is frequently talking to clients and updating them on the information they value.

You've also learned that the right mindset is beneficial for gaining referrals. A fixed mindset is an excuse-focused thought pattern stuck in the past. Past behavior portends future actions. In other words, if you had trouble getting referrals in the past, it is unlikely that you will keep knocking your head against the wall to gain them in the future.

A growth mindset is one of learning how to gain referrals by making mistakes. It is one of using setbacks as stepping-stones to becoming more proficient. A growth mindset focuses on never looking at a failure as forever. Instead it is only a learning experience to grow from in the future.

The results-focused mindset combines the growth version with a specific goal. If your outcome is to gain five referrals per week, you have to change behavior to meet that goal. Possibly you may want to memorize the three-month phone call, use centers of influence more effectively, or hold more client events. The real difference between a growth mindset and a results-focused mindset is that with the latter, you change your way of thinking in order to hit a specific result. A growth mindset means that you transform every setback into a learning experience. A results-focused mindset means that you will learn and adopt new skills and techniques in the quest to build your business with referrals. You will then apply those skills until you get the results you want.

Fixed-mindset people may attempt something but stop when it becomes tough. Results-focused mindset people will attempt something, then apply it until they get results.

The great basketball star Michael Jordan was interviewed on *60 Minutes* many years ago. At the end of the interview, journalist Steve Kroft challenged Jordan to a half-court game to see who could hit 10 points the fastest. As you might imagine, Kroft lost 10 to 0. Kroft asked if Jordan would let him win. He refused. Kroft then asked if Jordan ever lost. Michael Jordan said, "Yes, many times." Kroft then asked what Michael Jordan did when he lost. Michael Jordan said, "I keep playing till I win."

This is an example of a results-focused mindset. The only difference is that a results-focused person may take a break from playing the game to improve their skills, and then continue until they win.

You've also learned that the best way to getting referrals is simply to listen. People will always name-drop. They will always talk about their friends and colleagues. Comedian Woody Allen once said, "Eighty percent of success is just showing up." You need to show up a lot if you want to build a referral-based business.

You can show up even more effectively by becoming a great listener. If you listen well enough, you will be able to gain at least one referral in every conversation. When you hear a client name-drop, it's up to you to ask for more information. Ask for their contact information at the end of the conversation, so you can call the referred lead. This process is so simple that clients who listen during their own client conversations never run out of referrals.

In the next section, you learned what to say to referred leads in order to gain an appointment. You learned how to create an elevator speech, how to use the personal touch to engage the lead better, and how to learn more by using the five-step bridge. You also learned how to qualify a referred lead to make sure you don't waste your time.

Social media is a wonderful way of branding. It promotes you and builds exposure. But sales are never built on branding alone; they are built on relationships. While social media posts may be good exposure, your referral approach should be much more organized. LinkedIn makes that possible. As you call clients using the three-month phone call script, ask if you can connect with their LinkedIn connections. They will almost always say yes. LinkedIn gives you the chance to look at all the people your client is connected to. You then have the ability to filter people you would like to meet. During the next three-month phone call to your client, instead of a referral, ask who among the four people you've sourced from LinkedIn that they know. Clients will be familiar with 50 percent of their connections. Your job then is to ask the client to introduce you to their LinkedIn contact. This will minimize the pressure on the client to produce a name.

My coaching clients who produce the greatest number of referrals rarely ever ask for names. They listen for referrals, suggest names from LinkedIn, and get introductions from centers of influence.

We also spoke about getting the names of professional advisors on your three-month phone calls. Asking for the names of your clients' CPAs, EAs, attorneys, or any other advisor swill gain a constant stream of referrals. Most producers will call the professional and ask to develop a referral relationship. COIs are constantly bombarded by people asking for referral streams. Your goal is to make contact with the COI, talk face-to-face, and let them know what you are doing with your mutual client.

Tell the COI what you know about their practice. Ask specific questions about how they are growing their practice. In nearly every conversation, the COI will say "word of mouth" or "I don't know." Your job then is to suggest a client event (which you may pay for) in an effort to speak to the COI's top A- and B-level clients. You might also bring your top clients. This mutually beneficial event will book at least 65 percent of the attendees into appointments with you. It will also solidify the COI relationship, developing a constant stream of referrals in the future.

One of my coaching clients approached a CPA many years ago. He booked an appointment to talk about their mutual client. We know that 33 percent of CPAs want to grow their business and may be interested in a client event. Another 33 percent of CPAs have no desire to grow the practice and prefer to keep it exactly the way it is. Another third will want to grow their practice but feel uncomfortable with doing an event. These folks are likely to refer business to you if you keep in monthly contact.

One CPA said to my client, "I don't really want to do an event. But I would love it if you could be available during tax time so that I can walk my clients into your office. It would be better if you were in the building. Often I see problems with their tax returns and don't want to wait for another appointment. I want someone to talk to them immediately. I have an office available in my building. If you don't mind relocating during tax time, I will walk my clients directly to you for an evaluation. Are you good with that?" My clients who do this see their incomes increase by 50 percent. All from a simple COI referral relationship.

Divorce attorneys are another wonderful COI referral source. Often couples are in the midst of liquidating assets in compliance with a qualified domestic relations order (QDRO). They often have to sell the house, liquidate investments, split retirement accounts, and create liquidity in other ways. If you are there to help with these transactions, you will aid not only the attorney but the clients as well.

Divorce attorneys rarely keep in contact with their clients after the transaction. They don't really have a client base. They almost never market to past clients, even though a divorcee is likely to experience divorce again within the next ten years. Divorce attorneys are often referred, yet attorneys rarely ask for referrals. Since they are such bad marketers, a three-month phone call and tossing referrals to them will be a return source of business for you. You have to be very diligent and consistent. In my forty years as a business coach, I have rarely seen my own clients call COIs consistently. If they don't get reciprocal referrals within a few months, they lose interest in the COI.

My definition of a great producer is doing everything all the time. You have to be wonderful at marketing, posting social media, newsletters, speaking at events, and even submitting articles to magazines that your key audience reads. You also have to call both your A and B clients and your COIs every three months. Very few people have the self-discipline to do this. They would rather pay for poor quality leads, spend thousands of dollars for dinner seminars, and waste money using lead sources, which often producing very poor results.

You also learned about the Net Promoter Score (NPS). NPS is a way of measuring how referable you are. It involves asking how likely a client is to refer you to a friend, using a scale from 1 to 10. A low score means that the relationship is not strong enough to generate a referral. A high score indicates that you are sufficiently referable. But the score alone may not be enough. A follow-up question is necessary: "What can we do to improve our ranking for you?" Asking this and implementing the suggestion may be an easier fix than you think. It could be simply saying hello and goodbye as customers enter and leave your business. It could be more frequent contact. It could even involve a client's desire to talk without being sold to.

Finally, you learned about client events. The minicircle of Friends approach can be done weekly with any A- and/or B-clients, leveraging a few of their friends. You can do this at lunch, breakfast, or even over a cup of coffee. The Messina method involves asking clients to bring their friends to a bigger event. The incentive to bring friends can be a drawing for an iPad or anything else of value. You will book 65 percent of the guests into appointments, as well as another 33 percent of your existing clients.

The bring a name campaign (BANC) is another event. Here clients are asked to write down the names and contact information of people who could benefit by working with you. You will get far more contacts this way, although you will book fewer appointments than if the referral has heard you speak at an event. You can also use a guest speaker to draw even more people to an event. A best-selling author or another celebrity will generate a larger audience than would normally come.

If you use any one of these techniques, you will generate at least five referrals every week. If you don't generate referrals consistently, it's only because you have reverted back to a fixed-mindset way of building business.

Referrals are *it*. Introductions are the most effective way of building business that has ever been developed. The skills you learned in this book will make you more effective than will nearly every other lead generation method.

Most of your competitors can only dream about getting referrals. In fact, the Holy Grail in building any business is word of mouth. The fact that so few of your competitors have a system for getting word-of-mouth referrals is a testament to your skills.

Everybody wants referrals, but nobody knows how to get them. Now you know how to do it.

Make a referrals part of every conversation. Never let a client call go to waste without at least thinking about getting a name. Never sit on a referral for more than a couple of days. Call them asap. Always let the referral source know what you've done with the lead. If your client thinks you've ignored someone they've mentioned to you, referrals will stop, but if you keep the client in the loop, you will get a steady stream.

Although your clients most want to help their friends, they also want you to succeed. If they give you a name, they will actually help you sell their friend. Their introductory phone call will always be a positive. They will tell their friend how good you are and how much you have helped them.

But it all starts with making referrals a part of every conversation. Every speech, every coaching client, and every LinkedIn connection I make has a referral conversation built in.

When I book a speech, I ask for other regions of the company that could be a source of new business. I want to be referred to their colleagues. If I sign a coaching client, I want to know the company they work for and whether there is a speaking opportunity in the future. This is the results-focused mindset that you need for getting referrals. It's the thought pattern that suggests, "I wonder if there's a referral opportunity here."

These skills will build your business by 38 percent, guaranteed. Most of my clients have doubled their business within six months. These skills will work. All you have to do is apply them with a results-focused mindset.

Please contact me at:

kerry@kerryjohnson.com

Twitter: @DrKerryJohnson

LinkedIn: Kerry Johnson, MBA, PhD

Phone: 714-368-3650

Send me a note. I would love to hear about your results.

CPSIA information can be obtained
at www.ICGtesting.com
Printed in the USA
JSHW032329170621
15782JS00004B/5